Reading Celebrity Gossip Magazines

Andrea M. McDonnell

polity

First published in 2014 by Polity Press

Polity Press
65 Bridge Street
Cambridge CB2 1UR, UK

Polity Press
350 Main Street
Malden, MA 02148, USA

ISBN-13: 978-0-7456-8218-1
ISBN-13: 978-0-7456-8219-8(pb)

A catalogue record for this book is available from the British Library.

Typeset in 10.5 on 12 pt Sabon
by Toppan Best-set Premedia Limited
Printed and bound in Great Britain by T.J. International Ltd, Padstow, Cornwall

The publisher has used its best endeavours to ensure that the URLs for external websites referred to in this book are correct and active at the time of going to press. However, the publisher has no responsibility for the websites and can make no guarantee that a site will remain live or that the content is or will remain appropriate.

Every effort has been made to trace all copyright holders, but if any have been inadvertently overlooked the publisher will be pleased to include any necessary credits in any subsequent reprint or edition.

For further information on Polity, visit our website: www.politybooks.com

Reading Celebrity Gossip Magazines

For my parents

Contents

Figures and Tables   vi

Acknowledgments   vii

Introduction: Celebrity Gossip Magazines in American
Popular Culture   1

1   *Gendering Celebrity Gossip*   25

2   *All About Us: Celebrity Gossip Magazines and
the Female Reader*   44

3   *Stars on Earth: The Paradox of Ordinary Celebrity*   66

4   *Making Morality Meaningful*   89

5   *Ambiguously Truthful*   110

Conclusion: On Pleasure and the Popular   131

Appendix A Reader Profiles   138

Appendix B Editor Profiles   140

Appendix C Content Analysis of Female Celebrities in
Cover Stories by Age   142

Notes   145

References   150

Index   158

Figures and Tables

Figures

2.1 Cover story content, September–December 2009   48
2.2 Frequency of celebrity appearance by age,
    November–December 2009   59
2.3 *Us Weekly*, November 16, 2009   61
3.1 *Star*, December 14, 2009, p. 4/ *Us Weekly*,
    November 5, 2012, p. 26   75
4.1 Transformed Transgressors, *Us Weekly*,
    September 7, 2009, pp. 48–53   97
4.2 "Best & Worst Beach Bodies," *Star*, March 26,
    2012   103
5.1 The glory shot, the guilt shot, the grief shot;
    OK!, October 5, 2009/ *Star*, February 23,
    2009/ *Star*, February 9, 2009   118
5.2 *Us Weekly*, October 12, 2009   119

Tables

2.1 Weekly sections by publication   51
2.2 2010 Editorial calendar   52
4.1 Heroic vs failed mothers   95

Acknowledgments

I am extremely grateful for the many people who have supported my work on this project. Thank you to everyone at Polity, especially Joe Devanny, for his guidance and enthusiasm. Thank you to Helen Gray, for her attention to detail, and to the reviewers, whose thoughtfulness and fresh insights helped to shape this book into what I had hoped it would be.

To all of the participants who graciously contributed their time and personal stories, I cannot thank you enough.

Thank you to Wenner Media and American Media Inc. for allowing key images from *Us Weekly*, *Star*, and *OK!* to be included in this book.

Special thanks to my mentor and friend Paddy Scannell, without whose unwavering faith in the importance of this topic and in my ability to do it justice, this book would not exist. Thank you to Susan Douglas, whose knowledge, energy, and sense of humor proved invaluable throughout the revision process.

Many thanks to the department of Communication Studies at the University of Michigan, especially Robin Means Coleman and Aswin Punathambekar, and to the department of English at Emmanuel College for their continued support. Thank you to June Howard, for sharing her passion for magazines with me. Thanks to all of my teachers, especially Paddy Graham, Michael Joyce, and Karen Robertson, for their wisdom, wit, and encouragement, which has propelled me forward, even in times when I did not yet know where I was headed. To my family and friends, who have always supported me, believed in me, and laughed with me – thank you. And to Scott, for all his love, I am forever grateful.

Introduction

Celebrity Gossip Magazines in American Popular Culture

We see them in airports and grocery checkouts, lining drug-store counters and street-corner news-stands. They are laughed at, ignored, and purchased – skimmed, pored over, flipped through. Their hot-pink headlines proclaim news of dates and diets, breakups and baby bumps. Whether you thumb through them or thumb your nose at them, celebrity gossip magazines are a ubiquitous part of the current popular cultural landscape in the United States, and most other Western countries. Since their emergence in the early part of the twenty-first century, these magazines have gained popularity and power, earning millions of readers and dollars to match. But while a handful of scholars have considered the role of similar publications in other countries (Brewer, 2009; Feasey, 2008; Holmes, 2005; Johansson, 2006), little is known about the influence of American gossip magazines, despite the genre's cultural and economic prominence. What are these magazines really about? Who reads them? And how have they sustained their success during a socially and economically tumultuous period, despite the fact that their contents have remained remarkably uniform? This book investigates these questions, combining interviews with editors and writers, trade press reports, reader commentary, and textual evidence from the magazines themselves, in an effort to understand why celebrity gossip magazines matter in contemporary American culture.

Since 2000, a new crop of magazines has earned a place on America's news-stands. *Us Weekly, Life & Style, In Touch, Star*, and *OK!*, have become synonymous with celebrity gossip. Week after week, these colorful, photo-filled glossies reach millions of readers, peddling news of feuds and face-lifts. Celebrity gossip magazines are bright, colorful, and opinionated. Their stories are as short as their photos are large. And they offer bold headlines and oodles of juicy tidbits, for about the price of a cup of coffee. These features have helped celebrity gossip magazines carve for themselves a popular and profitable niche within a publishing market that has suffered through a decade of economic downturn.

The emergence of the celebrity gossip genre can be traced to the entertainment magazine *Us*, which in March 2000 announced that it would undergo a major redesign. In hopes of boosting lagging sales, *Us* transformed from a monthly entertainment magazine to a celebrity-focused weekly. *Advertising Age* dubbed the $50 million transformation "the largest re-launch in a decade," and Terry McDonnell, former editor of *Men's Journal* and *Esquire*, was named editor-in-chief.[1] The revamped *Us* promoted itself as a "cultural newsweekly," featuring celebrity news stories designed to attract female readers aged 18 to 34. Though critics cringed and initial sales disappointed, *Us Weekly* reported a 12 percent increase in circulation and a 34 percent rise in ad sales by the start of 2002.[2] Two months later, Bonnie Fuller, the Canadian media executive credited with spicing up *Glamour* and *Cosmo*, was tapped to replace McDonnell.[3] Fuller injected a dose of winking irreverence into the magazine, raking in readers, fueling a cultural obsession with celebrity, and transforming *Us* into an industry darling while earning herself the nick-name, "gossip's godmother."[4]

By the end of 2002, *Us Weekly* had increased its news-stand sales by 55.3 percent, more than any other mass-market magazine.[5] *The New York Times* proclaimed that "the medium has transformed the message," writer David Carr noting that the weekly's new format had converted scandalous tabloid themes into attractive stories, encouraging "thousands of new readers, some of them pretty far upscale."[6] Meanwhile, as *Advertising Age* praised Fuller for transforming the magazine into a "cultural touchstone," the maven made a controversial exit, leaving *Us* to become the editorial director of *Star*.[7]

Previously a paper tabloid known for its no-holds-barred celebrity coverage and *Enquirer*-style covers, *Star* was to undergo a glossy, 20-million-dollar makeover in order to compete with *Us*.[8] American Media, the tabloid's parent company, hoped that Fuller and her "upbeat," "energetic" spirit would place *Star* at the center of the growing celebrity weekly industry.[9] The industry was, in fact, expanding. As Fuller took her place at the helm of *Star*, Bauer Publishing debuted two new celebrity weeklies, *In Touch* and *Life & Style*, both featuring content, format, and aesthetics nearly identical to those of *Us*.[10] Then, in August, 2005, British media mogul Richard Desmond and his company, Northern & Shell, launched an American edition of the popular British tabloid *OK!*.

As the industry grew, sales continued to climb, silencing critics who predicted that the market was oversaturated and doomed to fail. In 2003, Janice Min replaced Fuller as *Us Weekly*'s editor-in-chief. The following year, news-stand sales of *Us* rose 47.3 percent to 745,887 copies per week and *Advertising Age* named *Us* 2004's "Magazine of the Year:"

> Roll your eyes; purse your lips and shake your head; slip it inside your bag so your smarty-pants friends don't see it. But resistance is futile. Thanks to its unprecedented fusion of newsstand heat, advertiser interest and – most incredibly – the way it's found a younger and wealthier audience, *Us Weekly* is *Advertising Age*'s Magazine of the Year.[11]

And *Us* was not the only one cashing in on the weekly craze. In 2006, advertiser spending in *Us*, *In Touch*, *Life & Style* and *OK!* totaled $564 million, proving that gossip could sell, and sell big, to the coveted female demographic.[12] All the while, countless blogs, television programs, and even newspapers were revamping their content in an attempt to court celebrity-obsessed audiences. By the middle of the decade, the celebrity gossip genre had become an instantly recognizable and virtually unavoidable part of American pop culture. "Like it or not," wrote *Advertising Age*'s Jon Fine, "*Us Weekly* has become a cultural reference point, if not an entire world view."[13]

Celebrity magazines have existed since the start of the twentieth century, when cinema captured audiences' attention and fueled fans' desire to learn about their favorite players. Richard deCordova (1990) traces the ways in which the discourse surrounding actors transformed throughout the nineteen teens and twenties. Early fan magazines such as *Photoplay, Silver Screen,* and *Picture-Play Magazine* produced what deCordova calls "picture personalities." Narratives within these publications emphasized the link between actor and character and essentially worked to produce the actor as an extended version of his or her filmic representation. As deCordova writes:

> Personality existed as an effect of the representation of character in a film – or, more accurately, as the effect of the representation of character across a number of films . . . Extrafilmic discourse did talk about the players' personalities outside of films but only to claim that they were the same as those represented in films . . . the player's identity was restricted to the textuality of the films she or he was in. (1990: 86–7)

The content of these stories was primarily controlled by studio press departments, which "operated not only as promoters but also as protectors," crafting public personae that fit with the studio's desired image, according to Joshua Gamson, who traces the history of the celebrity industry in his book, *Claims to Fame* (1994: 27).

But, by 1914, the discourse around picture personalities took an important turn. Whereas early stories were often redundant and narrowly focused, these new narratives began to explore the players' private lives outside of film, dramatically expanding the scope of information that readers could learn about famous figures. DeCordova argues that it is precisely this shift that produces the actor as *star*. Throughout the twentieth century, discourse around the star continued to evolve and expand. In the 1920s, emphasis on actors' private lives produced scandalous stories, wherein the stars' domestic problems and moral transgressions took center stage (deCordova, 1990: 119). By the 1930s, the glamorous aura of the star was dissolving; actors were now depicted not as idols or as democratic royalty, but as wealthier, prettier versions of ordinary people (Gamson, 1994: 29). As the studio system began to unravel in the late 1940s and early 1950s, due largely to anti-trust legislation and the emergence of television, actors gained greater control of their own image. Since then, an entire industry of publicists, agents, stylists, editors, and groomers has emerged to help stars cultivate and maintain their fame, a fame based not on some idealized screen image, but on the appearance of authenticity and ordinariness (Gamson, 1994). In 1974, these stars began appearing in the newly launched *People Magazine*, whose names-make-news approach to reporting helped feed an appetite for celebrity culture that has influenced the American media landscape ever since. All the while, a growing body of research has emerged in an effort to understand the proliferation of fame and its industries; scholars have examined the historical roots of fame (Braudy, 1986), the evolution of stardom and its ties to the development of radio, film, and television (Gamson, 1994; Marshall, 1997), the relationship between celebrity and commodification (Cashmore, 2006), and the ways in which star stories impact conceptions of social mobility (Sternheimer, 2011) and ethnicity (Negra, 2001).

In many ways, the latest group of celebrity magazines may be viewed as a logical extension of pre-existing discourses around celebrity and stardom. Today's celebrity gossip magazines have much in common with their predecessors. They emphasize the sensational and the outrageous. They revel in bias and speculation. They, too, use large, stylized images to catch the eye of potential readers. And they follow the rich and famous with a monomaniacal eye. Yet I argue that *Us Weekly, Life & Style, Star, In Touch,* and *OK!* can be understood as a singular cohort, one which marks an important elaboration and exaggeration of previous representations of fame. Throughout this book, I refer to these five texts as *celebrity gossip magazines* and I consider them a genre, in and of themselves. I do so not to diminish their historical ties to other similar publications, but to emphasize the common features and affordances of these particular texts.

What makes celebrity gossip magazines unique? First, the aesthetic of the genre is specific and shared across publications. As chapter 2 demonstrates, all celebrity gossip magazines adhere to a defined set of visual and textual codes. In particular, the use of many, large, full-color photographs is a contemporary development, one that has only been made possible thanks to digital imaging technologies and the widespread availability of high-speed Internet.

Second, where previous star magazines meshed industry-related content with narratives about the personal lives of the stars, contemporary celebrity gossip magazines eschew nearly any reference to players' professional careers. Here, celebrities are no longer idols of the silver screen. They are ordinary. They are, quite simply, just like us. The paradox of ordinary stardom is a theme that has been widely discussed in the literature on celebrity culture (Dyer, 1991; Gamson, 1994; Holmes and Redmond, 2006; Lai, 2006). But while the motif of the ordinary celebrity is nothing new, it is made all the more salient in the twenty-first century, in an age where the fame (and notoriety) once reserved for royalty, inventors, and film stars (Braudy, 1986; Rojek, 2001) has been sprinkled over a vast and ever-growing army of celebs culled from the ranks of reality television shows, YouTube videos, and human interest stories.

Celebrity theorist Chris Rojek calls this new crop of stars *celetoids*, "media-generated, compressed, concentrated" celebrities, made famous through pseudo-events and the industrial machinery of a well-oiled celebrity industry (2001: 18). The need for these types of stars has grown exponentially since the emergence of cable television in the 1980s, when the rise of niche channels and the 24-hour news cycle sparked a ceaseless demand for content (Lotz, 2007).[14] Further fueling this push for fresh faces, reality television took root in the 1990s and early 2000s with the debut of *The Real World, Survivor, Big Brother*, and *American Idol*. Now a pervasive part of our televisual landscape, reality TV creates a demand for new "ordinary" stars while simultaneously grooming an endless group of up-and-comers who, once known, are discussed in the tabloid press, dissected on talk and entertainment news shows, and obsessed over in the blogosphere. Add to this the rise of online technologies and social media and the explosion of "ordinary" celebrities on the pages of gossip magazines seems almost inevitable.

In addition, deCordova notes that early claims about the ordinariness of the stars were built on representations of private life, which typically focused on familial relationships.

Thus celebrity scandals of the early twentieth century emphasized breaks in the traditional nuclear family caused by infidelity and divorce. In short, moral transgression for stars of the past was defined as sexual transgression. In chapter 3, I trace the development of the ordinary star as she appears in celebrity gossip magazines; indeed, contemporary narratives continue to emphasize family life – marriages, babies, and the like – and today's scandals are often sexual in nature. Yet within contemporary narratives, a new site of moral transgression emerges. Private life, and the codes of conduct deemed "ordinary" therein, is no longer defined only by sexual relations, but also by the body and the regimentation of that body (Douglas, 2010). The culmination of sexual and bodily discourses of the private appears in what is perhaps the genre's defining narrative: the baby bump watch. As we will see in chapter 4, this storyline obsessively scrutinizes the female body (which, being pregnant, is also a sexual body). The genre's emphasis on the behaviors and bodies of *women* is crucial, for the final element that distinguishes celebrity gossip magazines from fan magazines of the past is their singular focus on female stars and female life.

Celebrity gossip magazines are fundamentally concerned with the experiences and emotions of women. Although each publication has a self-avowed mission: to combine "honest and accurate reporting" with a "fun, irreverent format" (*In Touch*), to "highlight Hollywood's timeliest trends and help readers translate their favorite stars' styles into their own lives" (*Life & Style*), or to be "the magazine the stars trust" (*OK!*), all share a single-minded goal: to document and comment on the personal lives of celebrity women. In other words, these magazines are not simply about famous *figures*; they are about famous *females*.

This is not to say that male celebrities do not appear in the pages of these magazines. They do. However, they are featured less often and less prominently than their female counterparts. They are rarely the centerpiece of a story and narratives are almost never told from a male perspective. To see this, we need only think of the British royal family. Prince William, Duke of Cambridge, is, as the heir to the British throne, arguably the most renowned man in England. And yet when he appears in the pages of celebrity gossip magazines (yes, even the American ones) he is not depicted as a famous figure in his own right. He is the son of Diana, Princess of Wales (whom the tabloid press notoriously pursued), and the husband of Duchess of Cambridge Kate Middleton. Now, he is also the father of a mini-royal, Prince George. And so the Duke of Cambridge appears as a man whose import is determined by his relationship to the women in his life, not by his own prestige or actions. The role that men play across the celebrity gossip genre is that of support-ing actor.

Meanwhile, women take center stage. The faces of female celebrities, in various stages of jubilation and defeat, beam out at us from the covers of these magazines. Headlines herald the excitement and tragedy of female life. From break-ups to baby bumps, dates to diets, friendships to feuds, these magazines investigate and celebrate women's triumphs and challenges, all narrated from a female point of view. These magazines tell star stories, stories that have long been told about the rich and famous, but they do so in a way that specifically speaks to the experiences and concerns of women. *Reading Celebrity Gossip Magazines* is, therefore, not only a study of fame and an industry that both perpetuates and benefits from it, but is also a study of the ways in which ideas about fame influence ideas about femininity. Further, because this narrative emphasis, as chapter 2 will demonstrate, works to attract a predominantly female audience, this book takes as its starting point the idea that celebrity gossip magazines are a form of women's popular culture.

Loving (and Hating) Celebrity Gossip

I began my study of celebrity gossip magazines as a fan of the genre. While working at a museum in suburban New York, my female coworkers and I would spend our breaks and lunch hours debating the merit (or tragedy) of Jessica Simpson's frocks, or empathizing with Jennifer Aniston, or worrying over Kristen Stewart and her angsty expressions. We were often most intrigued, however, by the genre's depic-tion of pregnancy – from the so-called "bump patrol," relent-lessly eyeing celebrity midsections, to tales of Nadya Suleman, aka "Octomom," who was notorious for giving birth to octuplets in 2009, to, my personal favorite, a story entitled *Bagel or Baby?*, which wondered aloud whether a particular starlet was with child, or had simply consumed a carb-heavy breakfast.

I was particularly struck, and troubled, by the genre's depiction of Nicole Richie. A fan of Nicole since her performance in the reality show *The Simple Life*, I had watched the magazines attack her for her weight (first too heavy, then too thin), her alleged drug use, and her run-ins with police. But then, in 2007, a magical thing happened – or so the magazines would have us believe – Nicole Richie became pregnant. No longer portrayed as an anorexic party girl, Nicole had transformed into a bubbly earth mother complete with goddess gowns and arm jewelry.

Nicole was one of the first celebrity women, but certainly not the last, to undergo such a mommy makeover in the celebrity gossip press. This transformation narrative, a kind of contemporary fairy tale, was the starting point for my research. I tracked the magazines' portrayals of pregnancy and discovered that mothers were either presented as heroes, failures, or, like Nicole, transformed transgressors. These pregnancy narratives seemed to lay out a specific set of narrow, heteronormative rules and moralities for how to be a good mother, and thereby a good woman, in contemporary American culture. Famous moms-to-be who didn't abide by these rules were cast as selfish, reckless, and unattractive.

But while this research revealed much about the ideological messages embedded in celebrity gossip narratives, it did little to explain why women, even those media-savvy women with whom I'd worked, including self-avowed feminists like myself, continue to seek out, read, and enjoy these texts. What I found as a scholar was quite different from what I had enjoyed as a fan. Once eager to read the magazines, I was now disheartened. Here were images of mindless women, obsessed with overpriced shoes, unfaithful men, and plastic surgery. Here the shame of cellulite, the success and (more frequent) failure of heterosexual romance, and the joys of motherhood, were neurotically discussed, week after week. Here were magazines about some of the most professionally successful, economically influential, and culturally powerful women in the world, and all we could talk about was their latest trip to Jamba Juice? Something, I thought to myself, was seriously wrong here.

To better understand the duality of my researcher–reader position, I turned to other feminist media scholars who had come before me. I was particularly moved by the work of Janice Winship, whose 1987 book, *Inside Women's Magazines*, critically examines the ways in which popular magazines teach their readers important lessons about gender. In the book's preface, Winship reflects on her own position as feminist, scholar, and reader:

> On and off I've been doing research on women's magazines since 1969, originally for an undergraduate dissertation and then for a PhD. For about the same number of years I've also thought of myself as a feminist. It was never easy, however, to integrate those two concerns . . . 'Surely we all know women's magazines demean women and solely benefit capitalist profits. What more is there to say?' I experienced myself as a misfitting renegade who rarely dared to speak up for magazines, however weakly.
>
> Yet I continued to believe that it was as important to understand what women's magazines were about as it was, say, to understand how sex discrimination operated in the workplace. I felt that to simply dismiss women's magazines was also to dismiss the lives of millions of women who read and enjoyed them each week. More than that, *I* still enjoyed them, found them useful and escaped with them. And I knew I couldn't be the only feminist who was a 'closet' reader. (1987: xii)

Indeed, Winship is not alone. In her 1994 book, *Where the Girls Are: Growing Up Female with the Mass Media*, feminist cultural critic Susan Douglas comments on her own conflicted experience:

> When I open *Vogue*, for example, I am simultaneously infuriated and seduced, grateful to escape temporarily into a narcissistic paradise where I'm the center of the universe, outraged that completely unobtainable standards of wealth and beauty exclude me and most women I know from the promised land. I adore the materialism; I despise the materialism. I yearn for self-indulgence; I think the self-indulgence is repellent. I want to look beautiful; I think wanting to look beautiful is about the most dumb-ass goal

you could have. The magazine stokes my desire; the magazine triggers my bile. And this doesn't only happen when I'm reading *Vogue*; it happens all the time . . . On the one hand, on the other hand – that's not just me – that's what it means to be a woman in America. (1994: 9)

These authors' words reassured me that my own double-edged relationship with gossip magazines was not some kind of bizarre anomaly, but a tension that has motivated feminist media scholars to turn a critical eye on the popular texts that simultaneously attract and outrage us. And, indeed, as I would come to learn in speaking with readers, women outside of the academy often feel this uneasy tension in their everyday lives.

Looking back, I realize now that my inability to register my affection for celebrity gossip in light of my textual findings stemmed from deep-seated assumptions. As a media scholar, I had been taught to look to the text. This is precisely where I began my investigation and, perhaps unsurprisingly, I arrived at the conclusion that many before me had also reached. What I found in celebrity gossip magazines were themes of patriarchy, ideology, stereotypes, and problems. But my problematization of celebrity magazines was not a personal epiphany. Rather, it was an effort to apply long-standing critiques of popular culture, which I had been taught and subsequently adopted.

The type of ideology critique that I engaged in is indicative of the academic study of popular culture in general, and women's popular culture in particular. Early scholarship in the field of mass communication was riddled with an academic worry over how "ordinary people" would deal with the problem of the popular (Scannell, 2007). Scholars working in the Frankfurt School tradition dubbed the popular "mass culture," and argued that popular forms of entertainment were inauthentic distractions, ideological traps. By the 1960s, Richard Hoggart and Raymond Williams had begun to push back against the assumption that "mass culture" was inherently bad, making a claim for the value of the ordinary and the everyday. Hoggart and Williams argued that culture is not the province of the elite (the opera, the ballet, the sonnet), but rather the fabric of everyday life (the local custom, the inside joke, the neighborhood pub), a thread that "pervades all human artifacts and practices" (Scannell, 2007: 114). Their work laid a foundational path, debunking the authority of *official culture* and paving the way for the emerging field of cultural studies.

During the 1970s and 1980s, as second-wave feminist scholarship grew up in academia, feminist media scholars took up the project of the popular, with a specific focus on female audiences. Writers such as Angela McRobbie, Lynn Spigel, and Charlotte Brunsdon fought to gain recognition for the popular music, magazines, and television programs that mattered to women and to justify the value of the academic study of those texts. Since that time, feminist media scholars have examined the production (D'Acci, 1994), content (Coward, 1985; Douglas, 1994; Warwick, 2007; Winship, 1987), and audience reception (Brunsdon, 1978; Hobson, 1980; Morley, 1986) of popular texts. This body of research reflects a tension between a desire to recognize and take seriously the interests and concerns of women and a critical awareness of the way in which the cultural products consumed by women often seem to encourage retrograde representations of gender and frustrate feminist goals.

But while some scholars have acknowledged the paradoxical relationship that female audiences have with the popular feminine texts they love (or love to hate), the academic feminist position on women's popular culture has often been mired in a desire to critique the ideological messages embedded in these texts. At the leading edge of the second-wave feminist movement, Betty Friedan's classic book, *The Feminine Mystique* (1963/1974), warned of the dangers of popular women's magazines. Since that time, many feminist scholars have focused their attention on the negative aspects of these texts, arguing that they present a narrow, stereotypic, or conservative view of women and their social roles, and therefore have the potential to stymie women's social and political progress (Ballaster et al., 1991; Ferguson, 1983; Tuchman, 1978). Scholars working within this critical framework claim that celebrity gossip magazines rely upon and reproduce narrow versions of normative femininity and point to necessarily problematic features of contemporary mass culture. But, like my own initial critique, many of these arguments are grounded in textual analysis and rarely account for audience interpretation.

While this body of work provides valuable insight into the power, and potential problems, of media messages, it stops short of explaining the appeal of popular texts. Why, if women's popular culture is so bad for us, do we continue to seek it out and enjoy it? Are we masochists, or simply dupes? I do not consider myself either; nor do my friends and colleagues who enjoy *Us Weekly*, Taylor Swift, and the occasional episode of *The Real Housewives*. These ideology critiques, then, do not help to explain the meanings and values of these texts within our popular culture; nor do they explain what audiences do with these texts. As Ien Ang writes in her discussion of the television soap opera *Dallas*, these types of content analyses often lead to a condemnation of women's popular culture as "reinforcers of the patriarchal status quo and the oppression of women" (1985: 119). In order to avoid such critiques, *Reading Celebrity Gossip Magazines* makes a distinction between *representations* of femininity and the *practices* that female audiences employ to make sense of those representations, acknowledging that audiences' meaning-making processes are rarely, if ever, acts of careless acceptance.

Within the literature on women's popular culture, two texts stand out for their willingness to confront the troubling tension between ideology and pleasure that resounds throughout the field of feminist media studies: Janice Radway's *Reading the Romance* and Joke Hermes' *Reading Women's Magazines*. These works have informed my theoretical and methodological approach to the study of celebrity gossip magazines, as well as the title of this book.

In her 1984 study of romance novel readers, Radway, a feminist, begins with the assumption that romances are ideologically problematic for her readers. But what she finds is that the women whom she interviews are not ideological dupes, but rather conscious, active audiences with specific tastes and motivations. Ultimately, Radway concludes that it is the act of reading, the process and the purpose, which produces pleasure for her readers. And while the romance is a fixed text with many identifiable and indelible features, and while the reading of the romance is indeed dependent on those features, Radway recognizes that an examination of the text alone does not allow her to fully understand the meaning of the text in the lives of its readers. In the 1991 reissue of the book, Radway acknowledges that her original analysis was colored by her own academic background and motivations, and calls for an approach to cultural inquiry that merges textual and audience studies (1991: 5–6).

Like Radway, Hermes emphasizes a combined approach to the study of popular culture; however, she goes on to argue for the positioning of cultural studies within the context of everyday life. Hermes is particularly interested in how texts are made meaningful, "the process of making sense of a text by recognizing and comprehending it and assigning it associative signification . . . as well as giving it a place in one's knowledge and world views." This meaning-creation "consists not only of cognitive thought processes, but also of a reader's imaginative response and the practical and/or emotional and fantasy uses to which she or he anticipates putting the text" (1995: 7). Hermes strives to privilege the meaning-making processes of her readers in order to understand how they make sense of women's magazines in their everyday lives.

In order to advance our understanding of celebrity gossip magazines, this book draws upon the strategies put forth by Radway and Hermes. *Reading Celebrity Gossip Magazines* acknowledges and points to the ways in which these texts traffic in particular codes of femininity, but it is not satisfied that these representations tell us all there is to know. This study looks to the texts themselves, but also beyond them, to the act of reading and to the role that reading plays in the everyday lives of readers, in order to understand how audiences make meaning from and take pleasure in their textual engagement.

Pleasure is, indeed, a core tenet of this project. In her study, Ang takes the "admission of the reality of pleasure" as her starting point and organizes her investigation around a desire "to understand this pleasure, without having to pass judgment on whether *Dallas* is good or bad, from a political, social or aesthetic point of view" (1985: 12). Bracketing these judgments, Ang is able to raise, and answer, critical questions about the nature of soap opera viewing. This study follows Ang's lead in an effort to understand how it is that celebrity gossip magazines present themselves, and are experienced by readers, as pleasurable texts.

To consider the question of pleasure is not to assume some singular female audience. Nor is it to allege that every element of these texts will appeal to all women or address some kind of monolithic desire that all women have. Rather, it is to acknowledge that these texts really do give us pleasure, and to take that pleasure, as Ang suggests we must, as the starting point for a very real and very necessary inquiry into why it is, and how it is, that our engagement with these texts gives us joy. This inquiry is particularly important when we consider the ways in which female pleasure has been and continues to be discursively constructed as a pleasure that is illicit, "less-than," or otherwise guilty. As chapter 1 demonstrates, the relationship between women and popular culture – the pleasures that women find in popular texts and the ways in which female pleasure genders those texts – deeply shapes the range of cognitive and emotional reactions that are available to us, regardless of our gender.

By attending to the question of pleasure in its own right, by focusing our attention on the *love* side of our love–hate relationship with celebrity gossip magazines, we can begin to answer the following critical questions. Why is it that these magazines have become so popular, especially amongst female readers? What pleasures do the magazines offer? Are these pleasures specific to the experience of reading celebrity gossip? If we feel guilty about enjoying these texts, where do these feelings of guilt come from? How do audiences exert control over their reading habits in order to enhance their enjoyment? And why is it that women, even those women who reject the codes of femininity that the genre has to offer, remain faithful readers?

Within the field of celebrity studies, Joshua Gamson's research most clearly addresses the multiple ways in which audiences derive pleasure from celebrity texts. Gamson sets out a typology of celebrity-watching audiences, drawn from focus-group interviews, wherein he details the ways in which audiences' varying degrees of knowledge about and acceptance of the celebrity industry impact their motivations for seeking out celebrity texts, the modes of engagement they prefer, and the satisfaction that they derive from those texts (1994: 146). This typology is crucial for three reasons. First, it clearly demonstrates the fact that audiences' approaches to celebrity texts are unique and varied, with many audience members only partially accepting or overtly doubting the validity of the texts. Second, it points to the fact that many audience members have a keen awareness of and are skeptical toward the celebrity industry. And, finally, Gamson's typology suggests that audiences can, and do, find different forms of pleasure in celebrity texts and that this pleasure is, at least in some ways, dependent on the individual's approach to and level of belief in celebrity culture. All three of these points clearly reject the notion that audiences simply accept celebrity media as an artless form and wholeheartedly embrace its messages. Gamson's work shows that many are skeptical of and take a critical eye toward their media engagement but that this critical approach does not produce an experience that is staid and sour, but rather one that results in varied and nuanced forms of pleasure.

Reading Celebrity Gossip Magazines takes up the question of pleasure in the context of celebrity culture. In order to understand the multiple ways in which the magazines afford their readers opportunities for enjoyment, this study looks to the production, content, and audience reception of the magazines. This three-pronged methodology takes up and extends Hermes' and Radway's call for a combined textual and ethnographic study, but adds an additional layer, also examining the systems of production that work to create the aesthetic and textual features of the genre. It is crucial, in my mind, to approach these three areas of inquiry simultaneously. Examining the magazines from multiple vantage points, we can achieve a deeper understanding of the text – how it works, what it consists of, and the choices that have been made to produce it thus. And, perhaps most crucially, we can begin to understand how, why, and to what end audiences make meaning from and find pleasure in these texts. Taken together, these elements provide a multifaceted view of the impact and import of the celebrity gossip genre in contemporary American culture.

Studying Celebrity Gossip Magazines

Over the course of my study, I obtained a year-long subscription to *Us Weekly, Star, OK!, Life & Style,* and *In Touch* magazines. These issues served as my sample, which I used to conduct close readings of visual and textual content and to inspect the standard practices used to present information within these magazines. I chose to examine issues from a single year in order to compare themes, visual and narrative tropes, editorial decision-making, and audience response across publications during a set time period. My decisions in sampling were also guided in part by the fact that most libraries (public and academic) do not subscribe to or maintain a collection of gossip magazines.[15] Even the publishing houses themselves, according to company representatives and employees, do not maintain a collection of back issues. For these reasons, celebrity gossip magazines become a kind of cultural ephemera almost as soon as they are produced; they do not have an archival home. In order to study the textual features of the magazines, it was therefore necessary that I obtain my own collection of issues. In an effort to demonstrate the ways in which the 2009 examples are representative of the genre's ongoing identity, this data is supplemented with gossip narratives that have appeared prior to and since the time of the 2009 sample.

Although this study does not focus exclusively on the textual content of the magazines, it does consider a careful examination of the text to be a critical element for investigation. Italian semiotician and literary critic Umberto Eco likens the text to a crystal which, once created, has a stiffness, a form that cannot be changed, and yet can be seen through many facets (1978: 4). Like Eco, I argue that a text possesses certain immutable traits (it is so many pages long, uses certain types of words, contains particular images) and that, while there may be multiple readings of a text, these traits shape and limit the boundaries of those readings in meaningful ways. It is, therefore, necessary to understand the structuring features of the text in order to understand the possible interpretations that it may generate.

Eco also argues that any text is produced for a model reader and that, in order for the text to be effective, it must communicate to that reader. In chapter 2, I characterize the celebrity gossip magazine's model reader and show how the genre works to directly hail that reader. The relationship between text and reader is crucial because, as Eco writes, "the exactness of the textual project makes for the freedom of the Model Reader" (1978: 10). That is to say, the specific nature of the text allows for a variety of reading experiences and interpretations. Celebrity gossip magazines are exact texts; the stories they tell, the images they highlight, and the aesthetics they value are highly uniform. By examining these features in greater detail, we can understand how they produce the genre's model reader and what types of interpretive possibilities they afford that reader.

My analysis of the text is also informed by conversations with editors, who provided insight into the magazines' production process. In the spring of 2010, I conducted a series of in-depth interviews with six former and current staff members at *Us Weekly*, *Star*, *Life & Style*, and *OK!* and toured the offices of *Us Weekly*. All of the editors who participated in this study agreed to be interviewed and to have those interviews digitally recorded. Throughout this book, I have tried to quote, rather than paraphrase, participant responses in order to provide a faithful account of their explanations. Whenever possible, I conducted follow-up interviews and member checks with participants to ensure that I was correctly representing their views. In addition to the information provided in my original interviews, I draw from data made public through reports and interviews published in the trade press. Publisher statistics, available via the magazines' online media kits, were also instrumental in documenting trends in circulation and demographics. Taken together, these resources allowed me to triangulate the information provided by editors and to ensure consistency and accuracy.

Through an examination of the production of celebrity gossip magazines, we begin to see how these texts function – how (and why) they look the way they do, say the things they say, and appeal to audiences. This type of media production study, as Mayer, Banks, and Caldwell write, seeks to

"understand how people work through professional organi-
zations and informal networks to form communities of
shared practices, languages, and cultural understandings of
the world" (2009: 2). *Reading Celebrity Gossip Magazines*
looks to the shared meaning-making practices of profession-
als working in the magazine publishing industry in an effort
to critically evaluate the editorial processes that shape the
genre. These publications reach millions of readers each
week; by uncovering the assumptions, tools, and techniques
used within the industry, we can better understand the ways
in which these texts reflect, refract, and respond to our contemporary cultural values. Through this examination, we
also see the strategies editors use to make these texts attractive and enjoyable to audiences and can compare how the
industry's intended messages both consider and contrast with
audiences' real-world reading experiences.

This book, therefore, places industry perspectives in conversation with reader responses, drawing from in-depth individual and focus-group interviews with 11 female celebrity
gossip magazine readers, all of whom work together at a
museum in suburban New York, which I will call the Cube.
I chose to interview these particular readers for a number of
reasons. First, I felt it critical to speak with women. While it
is true that a portion of the genre's readership is male (between
15 and 30 percent, depending on the magazine and date of
issue),[16] the celebrity gossip genre is a feminine arena: its
readers are presumed to be female and its content is aimed
at a female audience. My goal was to discern how it is that
these texts come to be recognized within the popular discourse as texts that are "for women." I also wanted to
understand how these magazines present themselves as
"female," how they aim to (and, indeed, successfully do)
attract women readers, and how it is that these readers make
sense of the magazines despite, at times, disagreeing with the
images of femininity in which they traffic. So while the study
of male audiences who engage with female-oriented texts is
an important area of research – Hermes describes the practices of such readers in her study of women's magazines – and
while more work must be done, particularly around contemporary genres, in order to more fully understand how men
(and women) engage with and make meaning from texts that

are not, so to speak, "for them," this line of inquiry lies outside the realm of this study.

I chose to interview the Cube women, in particular, because I knew that many of them were regular readers of celebrity gossip. As a former employee at the Cube, I was familiar with the reading habits of the staff and the access that they had to these magazines; recent issues were left on tables and bookshelves in the staff lounge and other common areas throughout the museum. I later learned that the availability of the magazines was facilitated by one particular employee, Nina, who was an avid subscriber. Nina, who declined to be interviewed for this study, would read the magazines at home and then leave them in the lounge for others to enjoy.

The staff lounge at the Cube is an important site, because it is here that much of the Cube women's reading takes place. Further, it is here, during lunch hours and break times, that they engage in communal reading sessions. During my visit to the Cube, I experienced first hand the intense discussions (sometimes humorous, sometimes passionate) that resulted from the readers' airing of personal opinions about celebrity stories in conversation with other women. Because I was eager to understand why and how the Cube women read celebrity gossip magazines in a group context, I found it critical to return to this site of engagement.

I also aimed to speak with women who were similar to the genre's model reader; the Cube's mostly female staff members, many of whom were between the ages of 20 and 40, fit this demographic profile. The participants in this study are not intended to be statistically representative of the genre's readership and were not sampled in such a way as to represent specific strata associated with that readership. While the women who participated in this study come from a variety of racial and ethnic backgrounds, and although ethnic identity certainly may influence the reading practices associated with celebrity gossip magazines in meaningful ways, this book does not attempt to make claims about the impact of race and ethnicity in this regard for two reasons. First, I spoke with 11 women and I do not feel that this sample is large enough to warrant conclusions about the meaning-making processes of entire ethnic groups. Second, a central goal of this project is to understand the plural and often complex ways in which reading practices are informed by and impact conceptions of femininity. I therefore leave the important question of ethnicity for future investigation. Nevertheless, it is my hope that the diversity of the Cube readers' marital, racial, ethnic, religious, sexual, and professional identities provides for a varied and nuanced collection of perspectives that other readers will identify with, regardless of their own intersectional identities.

For all of these reasons, I returned to the museum for a weeklong visit in May 2010. During this time, I spoke with readers, individually and in small groups, about their experiences with celebrity gossip magazines. Some of these women were former coworkers of mine, others I met for the first time; however, I consider all of the participants my equals and the interview process reflected this paradigm. Throughout this study, I refer to both readers and editors by their first names in order to signal that neither holds more or less authority than the other. In many ways, this project is inspired by the Cube women and their experiences – as readers, as women, and as friends. I aim to present their colorful, heartfelt, powerful stories and, in doing so, shed light on the ways in which celebrity gossip magazine reading can, and does, impact readers' lives in meaningful ways. These magazines mean many things to many people in many different contexts; this study does not claim to account for all of those interpretations. It does, however, provide reports from editors, readers, trade press, and the magazines themselves in an effort to begin to understand the relationship between celebrity gossip magazines and their readers.

An Overview

This book is divided into five chapters, each of which examines a specific element of the celebrity gossip genre. Chapter 1 begins by providing a brief historical overview of the longstanding debates surrounding the genre, situating celebrity gossip magazines within particular discursive frames and mapping the way in which these frames have worked to gender the genre in feminine terms. Here, I link celebrity gossip magazines to an array of other popular texts, which I call the popular feminine. These texts have much in common, not least of which is the fact that they have all been subject to pejorative refrains within both the popular and academic discourse. This chapter traces the way in which popular feminine texts broadly, and celebrity gossip magazines in particular, have been characterized, and thereby gendered, within these discourses and the impact that such characterizations have on audiences' ability to take pleasure in these texts. Reader reports suggest that the gendering of celebrity gossip magazines encourages both male and female audiences to distance themselves from the genre and produces the pleasure of these texts as a guilty one.

Through interviews with magazine editors, textual analysis, and reader reports, chapter 2 examines the ways in which celebrity gossip magazines function as women's magazines. Here, we see first hand how the texts are produced for a female readership. But the genre is not concerned with *all* aspects of female life; its narrative focus is precise and specifically aimed at the personal concerns of women at a particular life stage. Drawing from the theoretical framework set forth by Eco, I examine the visual, narrative, and rhetorical techniques used to produce the magazine's model reader, mapping the ways in which these narrative codes hail that reader as one of "us." These codes allow audiences to feel a sense of connectivity with an extended family of celebrities, writers, and readers – all of whom are female.

Chapter 3 unpacks the paradox of the "ordinary" celebrity, a motif which has become increasingly widespread in the twenty-first century and which is re-presented and sustained through celebrity gossip magazines. Drawing from editor reports and from an analysis of the visual and narrative treatment of celebrities within the genre, this chapter traces the ways in which normality is set as a standard of authenticity for celebrities. But the cloak of banality is not only valuable for the stars, allowing them to enhance their fame and likeability, it is also a key mechanism for the magazines, which position themselves as gatekeepers of the "real" celebrities in order to bolster their cultural import. Audiences too benefit from these depictions; readers enjoy narratives about the day-to-day lives of the stars, even though they are aware that these stories are highly mediated and often far from ordinary. Further, narratives about the personal lives of female celebrities help make those stars knowable to readers, enhancing the identification and parasocial interaction that audiences experience and encouraging readers to use celebrity narratives as a way of thinking about their own lives.

Chapter 4 asks why it is that female readers enjoy celebrity gossip, even when they take issue with the genre's conservative, heteronormative images of femininity. Examining the treatment of romance and pregnancy, this chapter documents the ways in which celebrity gossip magazines construct a fable-like moral world in which particular types of femininity are lauded while others are damned. Here, we see how the discourse of private life, once based on a critical evaluation of the domestic and the sexual (deCordova, 1990), has expanded; this discourse now also concerns itself with the documentation and regimentation of the female body, especially the pregnant body. The so-called norms in which celebrity gossip magazines traffic are not, however, unique to the genre, but rather a reflection and magnification of conservative notions of ideal femininity that are widespread within our contemporary culture. Reader reports reveal that it is the act of reading, particularly in a group setting, that allows them to break down these normative constructions and, through conversation and consensus-building, articulate their own values and ideals. This process of contestation and reinterpretation is one that readers find deeply pleasurable.

Chapter 5 untangles the question of truth in relationship to celebrity gossip, looking first to the socio-political moment in which the magazines emerged and then to the texts themselves. Despite claims to the contrary, much of the genre's content is, according to editors, based on speculation, opinion, or information gleaned through a process known within the industry as editorialization. Further, the magazines are designed to be interactive; readers are encouraged, through polls and direct address, to weigh in on everything from fashion, to appearance, to relationships. These textual features allow audiences to exert control over their reading experience, inviting them to actively disagree and vocalize their opinions. The ambiguous truthfulness of the genre further opens up the possibility of dissent. Because they function as ambiguous texts, the magazines provide readers with an opportunity to talk back to the narrow representations of women that are so deeply entrenched in our popular culture. Yet despite this twist, it remains unclear whether celebrity gossip magazines do more to undermine or uphold these limiting versions of femininity.

The concluding chapter looks to the future of the celebrity gossip genre, with an eye to the relevance of print-based narratives in a marketplace that has become saturated with up-to-the-minute, web-based celebrity content. Finally, this chapter draws from Ellis's (2000) notion of "working through" and suggests that readers use celebrity gossip as a way of managing the challenges and anxieties that they face in their everyday lives. The practice of weekly reading allows women to confront the issues that matter *to them* in a way that is non-threatening and ultimately pleasurable.

Throughout, I argue that celebrity gossip magazines play an important role, both in the lives of individual women and in our broader American culture. Despite their reputation as trivial fluff, these texts deal with issues that are seriously important to female readers. That they do so in a lighthearted way does not make the topics they consider less important, but points to a need that women have to deal with personal struggles in a way that makes those struggles seem more bearable. Celebrity gossip magazines are not only about famous couples and glamorous gowns, scandalous escapades and happy endings. At their core, celebrity gossip magazines are about the challenges and contradictions of female life. They are about the joys and sorrows, the fantasies and frustrations that American women grapple with every day. They are, in short, about us, and therefore deserve our attention.

1
Gendering Celebrity Gossip

In early 2002, Canadian magazine executive Bonnie Fuller became editor-in-chief of the newly made-over *Us Weekly* magazine; eight months later, with news-stand sales up over 55 percent, Fuller was named *Advertising Age*'s editor of the year.[1] But even while she was celebrated for her professional achievements, Fuller could not escape her magazine's reputation. "*Us* is 'a deep-fried Twinkie'," Claire Connors, Fuller's former colleague and entertainment director of *Redbook* magazine, told *Advertising Age*'s David Carr. Carr himself likened the experience of reading *Us* to "eating the whole box of cookies, or ripping the top off a gumball machine and stuffing fistfuls in your mouth."[2] Such analogies are not uncommon within the world of celebrity gossip. *Us Weekly* and its counterparts are often compared to sweets, fluff, and treacle. This rhetoric suggests that celebrity gossip is an excessive, addictive, potentially dangerous treat, offering too-tempting-to-resist pleasures that ultimately leave you sick to your stomach. As Connors puts it, "It's so bad, it's good."

Today, celebrity gossip magazines continue to be defined in these terms. But this discourse is not new; nor is it unique to this particular genre. The rhetoric that suggests these magazines are saccharine, trashy delights is indicative of a series of deeply held discourses, which circulate around cultural texts that are produced for, marketed to, and associated with female audiences. This chapter examines the ways in which such texts, which I call the popular feminine, come to be gendered within both the popular and academic discourse. By examining these discursive frames, we can begin to understand how the gendering of popular texts impacts our perceptions of those texts, the meanings we associate with them, and our feelings about the pleasures we derive from them.

The Popular Feminine

Celebrity gossip magazines are part of a broader set of popular cultural products produced for, marketed to, and consumed primarily by women. Soap operas. Chick flicks. Romance novels. These texts are not only linked by their emphasis on female life and their popularity with female audiences, but also by a set of discourses which are commonly applied across such genres. In both the popular and academic literature, these texts and the audiences who enjoy them are routinely delegitimized, trivialized, and problematized. In an effort to point to the way in which these texts are inextricably linked within these discursive frames, I use the term "the popular feminine" to describe popular texts that are associated with women and female life and that are subject to denigration based upon this gendered association.

I draw the term "popular feminine" from the work of Tanya Modleski, who, in her 1982 book *Loving with a Vengeance: Mass-produced Fantasies for Women*, examines three forms of popular culture "designed specifically for a female audience:" Harlequin romance, gothic novels, and soap operas. Modleski uses the term "popular feminine texts" to describe the objects of her study. But while Modleski is fundamentally interested in the response of female audiences, she does not insist that the audience for these texts consists entirely of women; nor does she argue that all women enjoy them. Likewise, I do not mean to imply that all women enjoy *Twilight* and *Cosmopolitan* magazine, nor do I wish to suggest that women are the only consumers of these cultural products, although many women certainly do find them entertaining. Rather, I use the term "the popular feminine" to highlight the way in which the *perceived* gender of popular texts impacts their meanings and value.

Popular feminine texts are inextricably linked with female audiences. And while these texts may very well have many female fans, the actual gender of their audience matters less than its perceived gender. In other words, popular feminine texts come to be understood as "female." For example, celebrity gossip magazines, in contemporary popular discourse, are gendered feminine. This is a point that ordinary people agree upon; however, it is an academically problematic one because it is difficult to empirically prove such a cultural assumption. Yet scholarship suggests that audiences do, in fact, form consensus around the gendered nature of popular cultural texts. In her 1995 study, Hermes' participants assume that gossip magazines are women's texts (gossip, too, being a presumed female pastime). Irrespective of whether there exist men who read these magazines, or ladies who loathe them, Hermes' readers associate the genre with women. Dorothy Hobson finds a similar distinction in her 1980 study of television and radio listeners; her participants suggest that different media texts belong to specific gendered "worlds" and demonstrate a preference for those texts that belong to the "world" with which they identify.

What is troubling here is not necessarily the fact that different texts may be associated with audiences of different genders, but rather the consistency with which texts that have been gendered feminine have been linked to a web of discourses that undercut their value and underestimate the taste and intellect of those who enjoy them. As an author of young adult literature, Maureen Johnson knows this all too well. In an essay entitled "The Gender Coverup" (2013), she discusses the assumptions she routinely encounters:

> When I hear people talk about "trashy" books, 95% of the time, they are talking about books written by women. When I see or hear the terms "light," "fluffy," "breezy," or "beach read" . . . 95% of the time, they are talking about books written [and read] by women. Many times I hear people talking about books they have not read – books they've seen or heard about. I hear their predictions about those books. And then I hear people slapping labels on books they haven't read, making predictions. Again, I hear the same things. "Oh, that's just some romance." "I'll read that when I just want something brainless."

The books in question? You guessed it. Written by women. And some of those books, I'll note to myself, are fairly hardcore and literary, and I'll try to explain that. "Oh?" people will say. "Really? I thought it was just some chick lit book" . . . Somehow, we have put books into gender categories.

These gender categories, as Johnson makes clear, devalue texts that are presumed to be feminine. Further, these categorical assumptions work to shame audiences who enjoy feminine texts by perpetuating a distinction between cultural products that are "for women," which are painted as illegitimate, and those "for men" which, by contrast, are bolstered. Thus, anyone, regardless of gender, who seeks out or enjoys the popular feminine is subject to its negative glare.[3] In order to understand how it is that popular texts, and celebrity gossip magazines in particular, have come to be gendered and how it is that this gendering renders the pleasures associated with these texts taboo, "less than," or otherwise "guilty," we must examine those discourses which work to marginalize and trivialize the popular feminine.

Negative associations between women and popular cultural texts can be traced to the nineteenth century, as Andreas Huyssen documents in his 1986 article "Mass Culture as Woman." During this time, as the Industrial Revolution produced major advances in printing and new books and periodicals emerged to meet the demands of a growing population of literate workers, serial novels and family magazines became increasingly popular with an expanding cohort of literate women. At the same time, these texts were condemned by bourgeois critics, who alleged that these forms of "mass culture" were unworthy substitutes for "true literature" (Huyssen, 1986).

The critiques aimed at the popular press were often gendered in nature; as Huyssen writes, "a specific traditional male image of women served as a receptacle for all kinds of projections, displaced fears, and anxieties (both personal and political), which were brought about by modernization and the new social conflicts" (1986: 52). For example, in an 1855 letter to his publisher, writer Nathaniel Hawthorne complained of "the damned mob of scribbling women" – popular female authors whose books often outsold his, reaching hundreds of thousands of readers. And 30 years later, prominent journal editor Michael Georg Conrad wrote that literature needed to be emancipated from the "tyranny of well-bred debutantes and old wives of both sexes" (Huyssen, 1986: 50).[4] In order to guard themselves against the threat of the newly literate population, elite men held tight to traditional high cultural forms, contrasting literature, classical music, and the avant-garde with a bawdy, feminine mass culture in order to assert the former's legitimacy. In this way, mass-culture critiques became inextricably linked with the devaluation of female audiences and female pleasure in turn-of-the-century America. Since that time, this ideology has been used to trivialize and marginalize everything from *Gossip Girl* to *Days of Our Lives*.

The critique of mass culture works hand in hand with the discourse of public and private life. It has long been noted that the things that concern women lie outside the realm of the political public sphere, which was originally and remains to this day largely the domain of men. The political sphere of the late eighteenth century emerged thanks, in no small part, to the growth of a newly literate reading public, the literary public sphere, which was forged in the early decades of the century. This reading public had two distinct strands: one oriented toward news and one toward amusement. The news-reading public consisted of men who read and discussed the news in their coffee houses and clubs, from which women were excluded. The entertainment-reading public included women of the new bourgeois social class who had time, leisure, and money to spend on magazines and novels, which they consumed in what Jürgen Habermas calls the "intimate sphere" of the bourgeois household ([1962]1989). Outside the home, men read to be informed. Inside the home, women read to be entertained. Politics, war, business – these are public matters, matters impacting what Habermas calls "the common good"; domestic, familial, and bodily matters – these are private affairs, and so, the logic goes, should be confined to the intimate sphere. This division between public and private works to produce a gendered moral economy in which the concerns of men are deemed weighty, worldly, and important, while the concerns of women are considered lightweight, domestic, and trivial.

This discourse relegates important social issues, many of which directly impact women, to the political margins (Fraser, 1992; MacKinnon, 1983, 1989). In her essay, "Rethinking the Public Sphere: A Contribution to the Critique of Actually Existing Democracy," Nancy Fraser argues that "there are no naturally given, a priori boundaries" between public and private concerns and that "only participants themselves can decide what is and what is not common concern to them" (1992: 129). Fraser uses the example of domestic violence to illustrate this point, noting that, until recently, "feminists were in the minority in thinking that domestic violence against women was a matter of common concern and thus a legitimate topic for public discourse" rather than simply a private, domestic issue (1992: 129). For Fraser and other feminist scholars, conceptions of public and private, which are unstable, historically and socially relative, and "affected by political powers and dominant ideological systems" have been employed to undercut a wide range of issues pertaining to childcare, abortion, and domestic relations, to name just a few, which deeply affect women's lives (João Silveirinha, 2007: 66).

Indeed, this was the rallying cry of second-wave feminists: *the personal is political.* This mantra challenged the rigid divide between public and private life by insisting that the discourse of the personal was a false construct, an ideological wedge used to relegate important social issues to the fringes of political debate. Feminist activists and scholars have since sought to retrieve these "private" matters from the shadowy realm of the personal and reposition them in the public spotlight; however, despite their groundbreaking efforts, public and private, personal and political continue to serve as powerful defining categories.

In her 2008 book *The Female Complaint: The Unfinished Business of Sentimentality in American Culture*, Lauren Berlant argues for what she calls an intimate public, "a space of mediation [often facilitated by the consumption of media texts, i.e., "the popular feminine"] in which the personal is refracted through the general" (2008: viii). Within the intimate public, participants are linked through a shared "fantasy" of communal engagement, based upon "an expectation that consumers of its particular stuff *already* share a world-view and emotional knowledge that they have derived from a broadly common historical experience" (viii). The promise of a female-centered intimate public is that it allows women "to feel that their emotional lives are already shared and have already been raised to a degree of general significance while remaining true to what's personal" (ix). In short, the intimate public emphasizes the personal, the commonplace, the pre-supposed historical and cultural conditions that shape women's understanding of their own experiences in a way that creates, link by link, an imagined, but deeply felt, sense of connection and community.

Furthermore, the intimate public serves as a realm in which norms, values, and attitudes about female behavior and experience are monitored and discussed, although this dialogue is not based on the kind of rational discourse that Habermas advocates. This model is a productive one in that it allows us to recognize and take seriously, on its own terms, the sense of commonality that women's popular cultural texts provide to their audiences and the potential for "realistic, critical assessment" (2008: viii) and endurance that mediated engagement can encourage. And yet the intimate public that Berlant sets forth continues to be "denigrated in the privileged publics of the United States," regardless of the fact that it provides a key "experience of social belonging" for many women (2008: xi).

Despite gains in education and employment, assumptions about women's relationship to the private sphere persist. Popular texts that document matters of personal life or address issues concerning the home and the family, the body, and relationships are routinely feminized in deprecatory ways. And while scholarship has shown that the popular texts that engage with matters of private life provide audiences with an important opportunity for identification, engagement, and discussion – a means of seriously grappling with personal challenges in a pleasurable way – these texts continue to be diminished (Brown, 1989; Feasey, 2008; Johansson, 2006; Radway, 1984). To this day, the intimate sphere is defined as both separate from and less important than its public, masculine counterpart.

Softening the News

We can see the operationalization of these assumptions about public and private life in the discourse of tabloidization, which circulates around celebrity gossip magazines, talk shows, and entertainment news programs such as *The Today Show* and *Good Morning America*. Critics accuse these news programs, which often feature human interest and celebrity stories, of degrading and "softening" (i.e., feminizing) mainstream news. These critiques are not new – debates over the alleged tabloidization of the mainstream press have been ongoing since the early part of the nineteenth century when the penny press emerged in the United States – but the clamor has risen in recent years, as stories about the personal lives of celebrities, once a rarity in mainstream newspapers, television, and news radio shows, have become commonplace.

Celebrity news is some of the most sought-after and widely consumed content in the country and mainstream news sources, struggling to stay afloat in a content-saturated marketplace, are now cashing in on the celebrity craze. Reporter, writer, and former *Us Weekly* editor Lauren Schutte argues that mainstream news has been forced to incorporate these stories, which have the power to reach mass audiences and draw big ratings, because to ignore them would mean losing valuable market share. In addition, the once seemingly self-contained celebrity world is increasingly seeping into legal, political, and otherwise public realms. A slew of stars, from Paris Hilton to Lindsay Lohan to Charlie Sheen, have faced serious legal allegations and even jail time, their notoriety transforming stale crime stories into sellable network news. Meanwhile, everyone, from the Terminator, Arnold Schwarzenegger, to rapper Wyclef Jean to reality show mogul Donald Trump, has dabbled in politics, with varying degrees of success. Politicians, meanwhile, are appearing in venues previously reserved for celebrities: presidential candidates tweet, blog, appear on *Saturday Night Live*, and even star in their own reality TV shows (think former vice-presidential nominee and family on TLC's *Sarah Palin's Alaska*). Thus, although critics of tabloidization insist upon divisions between different types of "players," such as politicians and entertainers, who, as P. David Marshall points out, "are made to seem distinctly different . . . the categorical distinction of forms of power is dissolving in favor of a unified system of celebrity status" (1997: 19). Celebrity news exists at the cross-section of public and private life, troubling the discourse which marks these two realms as distinct and immutable.

But the tabloidization debate is not only concerned with a distinction between public and private life; it is also tightly woven into another, related, discourse. Within Habermas's model, the debate that takes place within the public sphere is intended to be reasoned and critical in nature. Rationality is a core component of public life. "Hard" news, therefore, is based on facts and on a rational weighing and reporting of information. Serious journalists verify their sources, check their facts, and avoid overly emotional reporting at all costs. But reason only gains its supposed superiority in contrast to its foil, emotion. As morality scholar John Portmann writes, the Western philosophical tradition is suspicious toward emotions and views them as dangerous, potentially subversive underminers of rationality (2000: 176). Further, (male) philosophers within this tradition equate emotion with women and reason with men. Because the public-sphere model presumes a debate based on reason, the association between women and emotion has served to justify the exclusion of women from public life. Human-interest narratives, storytelling, and emotion are the core elements of "soft" news, and celebrity news in particular. These formats celebrate the ambiguous and the uncertain, flaunt their opinions, and revel in their own point of view; they are considered an anathema to hard news. "Soft" news is feminized, then, not only because of its association with private life, but also because of its emphasis on opinion and emotion, which are deemed to be the province of women (Aldridge, 2001).

Fears that the tabloid style is sneaking into the realm of hard news are, in many ways, fears that the division between a public, masculine world, based in politics, public affairs, and "fact," and a "soft," feminine world, of emotion, private life, and opinion, has grown precariously thin. As celebrity news draws attention to the artificiality of the public–private distinction and "soft" news highlights the way in which mainstream news media have a habit of breaking their own rules – increasingly trafficking in the celebrities, human-interest stories, and emotion-driven narratives they claim to despise (Kitch, 2009) – the discursive distinctions on which the alleged supremacy of "hard" news rests threaten to buckle and collapse. Thus, the tabloidization debate is not only about subject matter or style. It is about competing value systems and the ways in which these gendered value systems systematically work to devalue the "feminine" realm of emotion and private life while bolstering the "masculine" world of rationality and public affairs (Bonner and McKay, 2007; Johansson, 2006).

Contemporary tabloidization critiques are among the latest incarnations of long-standing dichotomies, which maintain false distinctions between men and women, public and private, rationality and emotion. These categories are divisive, suggesting that different genders share distinct, competing concerns, and reinforcing the supremacy of masculine values at the expense of feminine ones. Critics of tabloidization therefore contribute to a discourse that feminizes and trivializes popular texts, reinforces the supposed inferiority of their audience, and produces the pleasures associated with those texts as suspect and fraught.

Feminism and the Popular Feminine

But the marginalization of the popular feminine is not limited to the discourse of the intimate sphere or even to the clamor surrounding the alleged "softening" of mainstream news. Academics have also contributed to an understanding that the pleasure offered by popular culture is dubious. While ordinary people have viewed mass media as a form of entertainment and enjoyment, academics have seen it as a problem. Since the 1930s, when millions of Americans began tuning in to the new medium of radio, scholars have considered the question of pleasure – where does it come from, what effect does it have, and who gets to experience it? The conclusions they drew were often disheartening.

In her 1941 study of radio listeners, Herta Herzog asserted that the pleasure of radio was an illusory, compensatory one, functioning primarily to help housewives escape the drudgery of their own lives. Meanwhile, Frankfurt School critics Theodor Adorno, Max Horkheimer, and Antonio Gramsci argued that the pleasure of the mass media was a false one, designed by the culture industries to spread a political agenda (Scannell, 2007). By the 1970s, Stuart Hall had extended this argument, theorizing that pleasure was an ideological tool, meant to reproduce dominant ideas as "common sense." The question of pleasure, for its own sake rather than as a pernicious political mechanism, did not begin to be raised in earnest until the 1970s, when critics began to explore what audiences liked and why they liked it. Some of this scholarship, much of which grew out of the emerging field of cultural studies, examined the popular texts – the magazines, music, and television shows – that women and girls found exciting and enjoyable (Brunsdon, 2000; Coward, 1985; Hobson, 2003; McRobbie, 1991; Modleski, 1982).

But even then, an influential strand of feminist scholarship surrounding women's popular culture reproduced the aforementioned academic critiques, treating the pleasure of these texts as a problem. Critics have argued that female-oriented texts, and the pleasure associated with them, are problematic because they emphasize patriarchal values and insist upon repressive feminine stereotypes (Ballaster et al., 1991; Friedan, 1963; Ferguson, 1983). Although these critiques point to serious and noteworthy problems, they often fail to address the way in which audiences experience these texts. Ang summarizes the argument put forth by this school of scholarship, and its impact:

> Unfortunately, a lot of mainstream feminist criticism seems to be inspired all too easily by the paternalism of the ideology of mass culture. Especially in the case of the mass media, much energy is spent in obsessively stressing how "stereotyped," "role-confirming," and "anti-emancipatory" the images of women in the media are. This is usually the result of a content analysis that bears all the limitations of empiricist realism, so that the firm conclusion is reached that such images reflect sexist or patriarchal values. Combined with a mechanistic conception of the effect of such representations on the behavior and attitudes of women, this leads to a total condemnation of [the texts] as reinforcers of the patriarchal status quo and the oppression of women. Women are therefore seen

as the passive victims of the deceptive message of [the texts], just as the ideology of mass culture sees the audience as unwitting and pathetic victims of the commercial culture industry. In this context an ideological atmosphere arises containing an almost total dismissal of and hostility towards narrative genres which are very popular among women. (1985: 118–19)

Ang's analysis points to the three crucial problems posed by these types of critiques: they contribute to the discourse which insists that the popular feminine is bad and even dangerous, they fail to explain why audiences engage these texts, and they suggest that ordinary women are simply cultural dopes, unable or unwilling to recognize their own oppression. Alienated from the male world and told that their own interests are damaging and problematic, these critiques, however well-intentioned, leave women culturally bankrupt.

Some scholars who acknowledge the pleasure of the popular feminine find themselves attempting to justify this pleasure in political terms. Michele Barrett, for example, argues that feminist scholars must understand why women enjoy things that are "politically bad for them," not because she wishes to validate that enjoyment, but because she hopes to activate it in the service of feminist goals, to "widen the purchase of feminist ideas" (1982: 56). Although Barrett recognizes the importance of pleasure, she nevertheless views it as a political tool, suggesting that women's popular culture cannot simply be pleasurable for its own sake, but that it must serve a larger political agenda if it is to be meaningful. Ang wisely responds to Barrett's critique, asking whether or not the pleasure of the popular can really be made politically useful, but a deeper question remains unanswered (1985: 132). Should it be? Must pleasure be politically useful in order to be validated? Should we privilege the pleasure women find in feminist zines over that which they find in *Us Weekly* and *Life & Style*? Should *Star* strive to look more like *Spare Rib*? To answer "yes" is to ignore the way in which pleasure is multiply and dynamically located within a text, to overlook the fact that readers can take just as great a pleasure in debunking (or reveling in) the feminine fantasy of *Vogue* as they can engaging with a text that they find overtly political.

This failure to recognize audiences' complex and nuanced meaning-making practices contributes to what Hermes calls "a highly unequal relationship," a gulf "between the feminist [academic] and 'ordinary women'" wherein "feminists . . . speak on behalf of others who are, implicitly, thought to be unable to see for themselves how bad such media texts as women's magazines are. They need to be enlightened; they need good feminist texts in order to be saved from their false consciousness" (1995: 1). These arguments assume that audiences do not make conscious choices about their media engagement but are, rather, passive recipients of direct and powerful media messages, a century-old perspective that has largely been discredited (Campbell, Martin, and Fabos, 2013).

Most recently, feminist critics have developed the concept of postfeminism in an effort to grapple with post-second-wave changes in the ways women and femininity are represented in popular culture. The notion of postfeminism – its meaning and impact – has been the subject of much debate; however, Rosalind Gill provides a useful account of what I understand to be its core elements: individualism, choice, self-discipline and self-surveillance, subjectification, and the ability to make over one's self (2007). Scholarship that understands contemporary cultural texts to be postfeminist generally falls into one of two camps: it argues that these texts perniciously reinforce traditional models of femininity while offering audiences a false sense of empowerment (Douglas, 2010; Negra, 2009), or it suggests that postfeminist texts empower and validate "feminine meanings and competencies" (Feasey, 2006: 191). Although their conclusions vary greatly, both of these critiques, like those of the patriarchal ideology that preceded them, tend to rely heavily on textual analysis, arguing that the text itself is innately problematic (or promising). Once again, the emphasis remains on the perceived ideology of the text rather than on how it is that audiences make meaning from and find pleasure in that text.

Gendering Guilt

With all of these critiques ringing in their ears, it is, perhaps, unsurprising that audiences, particularly female audiences, are often eager to distance themselves from the popular texts that they enjoy. "The ideology of mass culture . . . does not offer a flattering picture of [fans]. They are presented as the opposite of 'persons of taste,' 'cultural experts' or 'people who are not seduced by the cheap tricks of the commercial industry," writes Ang (1985: 103). Women bear the brunt of these critiques because they are assumed to be, and in many cases are, the consumers of popular feminine texts.

In order to understand how it is that female audiences make sense of their pleasure in the face of these multiple, powerful discourses, which resoundingly suggest that popular feminine texts are bad, I spoke with 11 women at the Cube museum in suburban New York, all of whom self-identify as avid readers of celebrity gossip magazines. How do these women avoid being associated with the caricature of the mass-cultural dope and still find pleasure in the texts they enjoy? The readers with whom I spoke had developed what Ang calls a "strained" attitude toward their textual enjoyment, distancing themselves from celebrity gossip magazines even while discussing their enjoyment. The term readers most often employ to separate themselves from the genre's negative associations is *trash*:

Danielle: Celebrity gossip magazines [are] sometimes trashy entertainment.

Mary: I think they're all trash.

Cynthia: I would describe the magazines as trashy.

According to Mary Ellen Brown, this type of *trashing* works to characterize popular feminine texts as "that which ought to be discarded, a sort of instant garbage . . . superficial glitter designed to appeal to those whose tastes are ill-formed according to the dominant perspective" (1989: 174). Like many of the Cube readers, Danielle, a single, 33-year-old director, Mary, a single, 33-year-old manager, and Cynthia, a divorced manager and mother of three, are quick to dismiss celebrity gossip magazines as trash, despite the fact that they enjoy reading them on a regular basis. Other readers also characterize the magazines in negative terms, referring to them as rags (items meant to be used and then thrown away) or as addictions (unsanctioned habits that will ultimately lead to overconsumption and harm). One of the readers, Sasha, compared the experience of reading a gossip magazine to that of eating fast food:

> It's almost like the difference between a fine restaurant as opposed to Wendy's and McDonald's. [Celebrity gossip magazines] are like Wendy's or McDonald's. They have pictures to excite you. You see the picture of the burger with the pickles and, "Mmm, looks good, Mommy. I'll take that number 5." [At nicer restaurants] you sit down with a maturity about you. *Life & Style* is like McDonald's.

By trashing celebrity gossip magazines, the readers express an awareness of the texts' low cultural value and are thereby able to distance themselves from the negative associations attached to those who enjoy them. Audiences have been shown to engage in this type of distancing around other forms of popular feminine texts as well (Ang's viewers insist that *Dallas* is "bad," Hobson's participants call soap operas "silly"). Yet when audiences participate in this discursive trashing, they work to further perpetuate the discourse that undermines the value of the texts in the first place. Thus, *trash* systematically stigmatizes both the content and audience associated with popular feminine texts, reducing their cultural and economic power (Holmes, 2005; Johansson, 2006). Moreover, this rhetoric suggests that women, for women are the assumed audience of these texts, are passive, tasteless consumers, who, given a choice, will consistently select the most worthless products.

Some of the Cube readers argue that celebrity gossip magazines are "trashy" because they incessantly scrutinize women's bodies, pit females against one another, or present a stereotypic view of femininity that is seriously lacking in diversity and depth. These are important critiques, set forth by conscientious readers. However, much of the Cube readers' "trashing" reflects not a desire to scrutinize the content of the magazines, but an attempt to disassociate themselves from negative perceptions of the texts.

For many of the women with whom I spoke, the notion that celebrity magazines are trash stems not from a personal discontent with the nature of the genre, but from an imagined male critique:

Helena: Ugh, [my boyfriend would] be like, "That's crap." He'd say something like, "It's crap. It's a waste of your time. Why do you read that?"

April: I don't think my boyfriend would want to hear it. He'd say, "They're so stupid. I hope you didn't spend money on that."

Cynthia: Men would like looking at the bodies of the women but I don't think that they would find any other thing in there interesting. Men? I don't think so. Even if they do read them, they wouldn't tell anybody.

The Cube readers imagine the men in their lives dismissing gossip magazines as trashy, trivial, silly, and unworthy of attention, and anticipate a negative male response directed not only at the magazines but at any woman silly enough to enjoy or (gasp!) purchase them. Even those women who do not personally define the magazines in negative terms are highly aware of this discourse. The readers' ability to generate this imagined male response with ease and consistency reveals the extent to which they have internalized the powerful gendered codes that mark popular feminine texts as illegitimate and unimportant.

At times, the Cube readers' trashing of the magazines prevents them from recognizing their enjoyment of the texts. Readers experience an internal conflict: feelings of pleasure on the one hand and a desire to reject the source of that pleasure on the other. This results in feelings of guilt:

Stacey: There was a sense of guilt about me, like I really shouldn't continue to spin this in society. I don't really feel guilty any more. Well, I do a little bit because I find in the economy it's an extra little thing. On the food line . . . sometimes when I'm cutting back, this is the thing that I think, "Ooh, do I really need to get that?" But I do find that just for the hour or two that I get to flip through it and can pick it up and leave it there and pick up where I left off, that it's enjoyable.

April: It's kind of a guilty pleasure. Definitely . . . I would never pay money for it but if it's in front of me I'll read it.

Stephanie: It's not something that I'd buy. I definitely wouldn't buy it. But if I see it I would pick it up and check it out, look at it. That's why I hurry up and read it before I get to the cash register. Because I don't want to buy it. I'm not taking it home with me! But I'll definitely engage it if I'm in a doctor's office and it's there or in the staff lounge and I have time to spare. I'll pick it up while I'm waiting for my food to heat up. I guess there is a small sense of guilt.

Although they find celebrity gossip enjoyable and relaxing, Stacey, a divorced 37-year-old program coordinator, April, a 26-year-old supervisor and student, and Stephanie, a 33-year-old executive assistant and mother of three, associate the magazines with feelings of guilt. Similarly, Danielle expresses mixed feelings about reading the magazines; she fears that she will enjoy them "too much:"

> I don't buy them because I'd be surrounded by these magazines in my house every week if I were to actually go out and buy them. I just wait until they're on the table in the lounge and I get my fill. I'm afraid to take it home – not because I wouldn't like it. Because I would like it too much.

These women are not particularly apologetic about reading the magazines. What they feel guilty about is *purchasing* the magazines, an act they all avoid.

They are not the first women to feel this way. In her study of romantic fiction readers, Radway finds that "many . . . women feel guilty about spending money on books that are regularly ridiculed by the media, their husbands, and their children" (1984: 54). Why do women feel guilty about buying books and magazines that are interesting to them? Perhaps it is because the act of purchase establishes the buyer as an active, purposeful consumer and thereby makes that individual susceptible to mass-culture critiques. By not purchasing the magazines, the Cube readers distance themselves from the "silly," "tasteless" women who "actually buy these things." Therefore, the Cube women often seek out the magazines when they appear in public places, such as the staff lounge, the doctor's office, or the nail salon; they also pass copies between friends. They are not the only ones who engage in these negotiations; in 2010, every issue of

Us Weekly purchased was read by an average of seven people.[5]

Feelings of guilt are not only experienced by female readers. Asked to reflect on the reading habits of their male counterparts, many of the Cube women report that their husbands, boyfriends, and male friends are interested in the magazines, yet reluctant to admit it:

Stephanie: My husband picks them up if I have them around and he's like, "I can't believe you read this" as he's looking through it. "I can't believe you read this!" as he's going through the entire magazine. [Laughs].

Stacey: My boyfriend, he wouldn't admit this, he finds himself gravitating toward them as well. . . . I think my boyfriend will say, "This is such nonsense. This is ridiculous. Who are these people? It's so ridiculous that you even buy these." But in the same regard, he can't help reading them. Sometimes they have men in the magazines or they'll have them with no shirt on. My boyfriend will make a comment like, "Oh, I used to look like that in my younger days." And I think, "Oh, you do the same thing women do."

Mary: Sometimes my boyfriend will read them with me. He'll lean over and start reading over my shoulder and then take it away from me. He won't admit that he enjoys them. But he'll sit there and read through them. It's considered to be a girly thing. It's not a manly activity. If it was *Sports Illustrated*, he would be fine with admitting it.

Stephanie, Stacey, and Mary's partners have developed a nuanced and contradictory relationship with the magazines; although they vocally reject celebrity gossip, they are actually interested in it. The men's rejections, then, are not rooted in a personal dislike of the genre (in 2012, 24 percent of *Us Weekly's* readers were male and, according to Schutte, the pass-along rate to men is "enormous") but in an understanding that the magazines are "girly things."[6] Men are aware that these texts are "for women" and, therefore, view their own enjoyment as taboo, which prompts them to hide or explain away their pleasure.

For both men and women, then, the enjoyment derived from reading celebrity gossip magazines is flecked with guilt. The experiences of both the Cube women and their male counterparts speak to the fact that the pleasure associated with celebrity gossip is culturally unsanctioned, not primarily because of the magazines' content, but because of the gendered nature of the genre. The pleasure that audiences associate with celebrity gossip magazines, much like that of the soap opera or the romance, is a guilty pleasure because it is a female pleasure, a pleasure derived from the "highly feminized, and therefore despised, Venus's-flytrap of pop culture" (Douglas, 1994: 239). We see, then, that the popular feminine remains stigmatized; both men and women who find its offerings enjoyable still feel compelled to justify or explain away their gratification and experience feelings of guilt.

This chapter has traced the ways in which the popular feminine is subject to a range of discourses that work to trivialize female-oriented texts based on their association with particular "feminine" values. We should regard as suspect these voices that diminish, condemn, and otherwise render worthless popular feminine forms, for these critiques perpetuate divisions between men and women that are as false as they are long-standing. A crucial element of this discussion has been the acknowledgment that popular feminine texts are enjoyed by a variety of audiences, not all of whom are female. And yet the *primary* audience for these texts is, in fact, women. Thus, dismissals of the popular feminine have a disproportionate impact on female audiences. But despite their eagerness to distance themselves from "trashy" texts, women do enjoy popular feminine genres. How can we account for this pleasure in the face of the harsh critiques that this chapter has outlined? What is it about these texts that women find particularly enjoyable? The next chapter examines the textual features of celebrity gossip magazines in an effort to understand how these publications are designed for, speak to, and ultimately produce themselves as pleasurable to a female readership. How do these magazines provide an experience that is so enjoyable that it ultimately outweighs the negative glare of the popular feminine? The answer lies in the production of the text itself.

2
All About Us
Celebrity Gossip Magazines and the Female Reader

Celebrity gossip magazines are about who's getting married, who's with who, couples, weight. "I lost 36 pounds with this awesome deal!" Read the magazine and you'll figure it out! It's love. It's hot dates. Who lost weight? A lot of surgeries too. Did she get Botox? Is that real? Her without makeup! Babies too, lots of babies. Baby here, baby there. It's a lot about aging . . . There are women all over them. They have four women here, ten here. You have maybe one good-looking guy. It's just basically her and her baby. It's all women.

Helena, a 21-year-old psychology student

From Britney Spears's head-shaving, to Jessica Simpson's back-to-back pregnancies, to Duchess Kate's wedding dress, the stories that celebrity gossip magazines tell all revolve around the "private" lives of female celebrities. These stories are designed to appeal to a particular cohort of readers: women between the ages of 18 and 34, many of whom may be facing the same life choices and emotions as their famous counterparts. Through interviews with magazine editors and an analysis of the genre's visual, rhetorical, and aesthetic strategies, this chapter examines the ways in which the celebrity gossip genre constructs itself as a narrative realm in which female stars, female life choices, and female desires are central. In addition, this chapter also demonstrates how it is that the magazines hail female readers, stitching those readers into their narratives through the strategic use of visual and textual cues.

Producing the Celebrity Gossip Magazine

On a spring morning in May 2010, I enter an anonymous-looking office building not far from Times Square in New York City. Having been ushered through multiple rounds of security, I am led up an elevator into a large, white newsroom. Cubicles full of young women, busily talking on phones and typing on keyboards, line the aisles. A giant glass room dominates the center of the office, one of its walls plastered from floor to ceiling with covers that read "Destroyed by Fame" and "My Plastic Surgery Nightmare." I have arrived at the offices of *Us Weekly*.

Once inside, I meet Lauren Schutte and Sarah Grossbart, assistant editors who explain how, each week, a staff of "mostly young, mostly female" reporters, writers, and editors transform tidbits and snapshots into a magazine that is read by millions. Lauren and Sarah, who both earned degrees in journalism before joining the *Us Weekly* staff, describe work in the celebrity industry as hectic and fast-paced, but fun and communal. They recount their early days at the magazine, as they worked their way through intern- and assistantships to reach their current positions; they're now responsible for generating new story ideas, writing articles, and editing the "Love Lives" and fitness report sections.

Throughout our discussion of deadlines and interviews, photo shoots and paparazzi pics, Lauren and Sarah make one thing clear; the stories they report are not only about celebrities, but also about readers: their lives, their interests, their emotions. The magazine's title, they explain, refers to the relationship between readers, stars, and the magazine itself. *Us* is about "you and me" says Lauren. "We're a group. I think the magazine is everybody's story." But whose story is this? Who are *we* to *Us*? Do *Us* and other publications in the genre actually create the type of community that they claim to promote? And if so, how? As this chapter will show, *we* are female readers, tied together through our reading practices. *We* are further linked through an extended family of famous women, whom the magazines make knowable, and who are, like us, grappling with the challenges of female life.

In order to understand the genre's distinctive approach to its readership, it is helpful to trace the process through which the magazines are produced. All publications within the genre adhere to a weekly schedule: most of the magazines debut on Wednesdays and so the production schedule is highly organized in order to ensure that deadlines are met in time for printing. Lauren explains how this process works at *Us Weekly*:

> Every Wednesday we have a big all-edit staff pitch meeting where you pitch three or four of your best ideas in terms of news value for the week. The top editors and the editor-in-chief direct the meeting and then they'll have meetings where they decide, "OK, these things are newsworthy and they require more space so it's a feature. Whereas these things very clearly go towards 'This Minute,' 'Love Lives,' 'Hot Hollywood,' or other smaller sections." And then all of those sections have individual meetings with the top editors in which they pitch things that are specific to their section.

After major stories have been identified, staffers spend the next few days writing, editing, and waiting for content to be approved by section editors and the editor-in-chief. By Friday, 30 pages of the magazine are sent to the printer; these pages mainly consist of the smaller feature sections, which appear in every issue of the magazine. In order to ensure that the reporting is "as fresh as possible," staff members continue to edit major news stories and more in-depth features until late Monday night and early Tuesday morning, when *Us* sends its final pages off for printing. On Wednesday, the new issue hits news-stands and the staff begins again, generating ideas for next week's edition.

Editors are acutely aware of the kinds of stories that will sell and prioritize each issue's contents accordingly. At *Us*, Lauren and Sarah explain, the team has an innate sense of relevancy: which narratives appeal to readers (babies and diets) and which celebrities will move copies (at the time of our interview, it was Angelina Jolie, playmate-turned-reality-star Kendra Wilkinson, and the Kardashians). Their main goal is to appeal to their core readership: women between the ages of 18 and 34. In order to determine which topics are most important to these readers, staffers track their preferences: they read letters, follow online commentary, answer emails, and make note of how many hits a story receives on the magazine's webpage. Editors also rely on focus groups, conversational sessions in which selected readers provide feedback by answering questions and talking with one another about their reactions and opinions.

According to editors, audience response plays a critical role in determining which aspects of the magazines are successfully reaching audiences and which need to be adjusted or reconsidered. Susanne Rieth, who has served as a photo editor at *Life & Style, Star* and *OK!*, explains that, at *Life & Style*, editor-in-chief Dan Wakeford uses focus groups to decide what stories will sell best and topics that receive the most positive feedback in focus groups are often given special attention in upcoming issues. Across the industry, editors insist that their readers' interests and concerns determine which stories make the cut.

But a content analysis of 77 *Us Weekly, In Touch, Life & Style, OK!*, and *Star* magazine covers published between September and December 2009 provides a detailed picture of the way in which the genre attempts to hail their target readership and suggests that celebrity gossip magazines may have a specific editorial agenda in mind. Within this sample, romantic relationships, in good times and bad, emerge as the primary topic of discussion, with 42 instances of relationship troubles or breakups, 31 mentions of dating and romance, 31 stories about weddings and engagements, and 28 references to infidelity. Narratives concerning pregnancy, childbirth, and, less frequently, children receive a great deal of attention, with 34 stories addressing pregnancy and 28 reporting on childbirth and the lives of the children themselves. Self-image, weight, and plastic surgery (33) also prove to be popular topics, and while stories about physical and sexual abuse (10), illness and death (9), debt or other financial issues (7), and drug abuse (5) appear less frequently, they remain a noteworthy feature of the genre.

This analysis points to the specific way in which celebrity gossip magazines understand and represent their readership. The magazines' contents are tailored to address the concerns of a particular reader whose demographic profile is constant across publications. Women make up approximately 75 percent of the genre's readership; further, an estimated 50

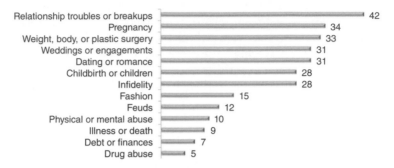

Figure 2.1 Cover story content, September–December 2009

percent of readers are women between the ages of 18 and 34.[1] A closer look at *Us Weekly's* readership paints an ever more detailed picture: *Us* readers have a median annual household income of $71,822, 68 percent are employed, and 69 percent have had at least some college education. While 48 percent of readers are married and 53 percent have children, many are single (38 percent). The median age for *Us Weekly's* female readership is 35 years.[2] While 75 percent of readers are white, 16 percent identify as Spanish or Hispanic, 12 percent as black, 4 percent as Asian, and 11 percent as "other."[3] And 90 percent of readers reside in a metropolitan core-based statistical area.[4] What emerges from this data is a very specific image of the celebrity tabloid reader; she is an urban, educated woman, typically white, who has a significant degree of disposable income.[5]

In addition, the editorial agenda of the genre clearly addresses a specific set of concerns and anxieties facing women at a particular life stage. These publications do not address the interests of teens (how to get a date, how to deal with acne) or of older women (how to raise adolescent children, how to manage a long-term marriage), but are tailored to females in their twenties and thirties.[6] According to the magazines' editors, women in this age range are very interested in reading about personal topics. "Weight, babies, weddings, any time we can get in anything like that, we'll do it," says Susanne, who reports that these types of stories are targeted to women between the ages of 18 and 40. Lauren agrees. "We definitely cover weddings, babies, weight loss. Those are all pretty major themes. If there's a cute baby, we'll run it."

According to editors, research and sales data suggest women are interested in reading about these topics and that, in presenting readers with these types of stories, they are, quite simply, giving women what they want. "What we've noticed is that women tend to be interested in women and not so much in men," says Valerie Nome, a self-proclaimed "fan" who used her fascination with celebrities (she auditioned for the Mickey Mouse Club at age 12) to launch her career as editor and red-carpet blogger at *OK!* magazine. "We tend to focus on fashion and weight loss, dieting, because those are things that women care about."

Celebrity gossip magazines emphasize multiple aspects of personal life, including parenting, fashion, body image, and relationships. It is, however, important to note what is absent; questions of career or politics do not appear here, despite the fact that these too matter to women. In short, these magazines ignore their readers' professional, political, and cultural concerns. Instead, their attention is tuned to a specific set of issues having to do with personal life: relationships, body image, children, and family. The editorial focus of the magazines cannot, therefore, only be characterized by its emphasis on women, but also by its attention to particular types of narratives that revolve around the personal choices facing women at a particular life stage.

Although many of the genre's competitors (*People, Entertainment Weekly*, various fashion magazines) do report on the professional lives of famous women and on the entertainment industry itself, celebrity gossip magazines rarely feature stories about matters of public life. This narrative focus, therefore, addresses a specific set of life concerns, positioning the magazines as a kind of Greek chorus for female readers and providing insight into important decisions – Should I get married and have a child? Should I leave my cheating partner? How do I feel about my body and my self? While they are not representative of the full scope of female interests, these subjects are nevertheless deeply important to many women, regardless of their ethnicity, education, or socio-economic status. Celebrity gossip magazines are created for and designed to attract those female readers.

When the Stars Align: Structuring Celebrity Gossip Narratives

According to Italian literary critic Umberto Eco, all texts rely upon "a series of codes," which work to make those texts communicable. In order to ensure that a reader will be able to interpret these codes, Eco argues, "the author has to foresee a model of the possible reader . . . supposedly able to deal interpretively with the expressions in the same way as the author deals generatively with them" (1978: 7). In other words, when creating a text, the author(s) must antici-pate a model or ideal reader who can understand that text. The authors (writers, editors, and publishers) of celebrity gossip magazines use a variety of techniques to create a text that effectively communicates with their model reader. Every-thing about the magazine, from how it looks, to how long it is and how many pictures there are, is the result of specific choices made with that reader in mind.

The magazines develop what Eco calls "an ensemble of codes" (personal pronouns, bright colors, large photos of female celebrities), which function as communicative tools (1978: 7). As they address the model reader, week after week, these codes also work to establish the brand identity of the genre; they become hallmark features of the celebrity gossip magazine. In this way, the codes of the text not only hail the model reader, but also work to create a product that is rec-ognizable to that reader.

Celebrity gossip magazines are highly recognizable and highly predictable. Not only do they draw upon the same visual and linguistic codes, but their content, and the way this content is presented, is consistent across publications and over time. All publications within the genre frame their nar-ratives using identical categories, as demonstrated in table 2.1. Each week, they transform a select handful of stories into *features*, cover stories which command between two and eight pages; the remainder of the magazine consists of themed

Table 2.1 Weekly sections by publication

Section theme	Us Weekly	Life & Style	In Touch	OK!	Star
Fashion comparison	Who Wore It Best?	Who Wears It Best?	Who Wore It Better?	Who Wore It Better?	Double Takes
Behavior judgment	Stars – They're Just Like Us!	Diva or Down to Earth	In Touch with Their Real Side	OK or Not OK?	Stars – Are They Normal or Not?
Photo stories	Hot Pics	Week in Photos	Up Close/Closer Look	OK Snaps/New Pics	Star Shots
Trends and products	Us Style/Beauty This Minute/Hot Stuff	Style Weekly	The Buzz/In the Know	OK! Buzz/Life on the A-List	Hot Sheet/Star Style/Star Beauty
Celebrity quotes	Loose Talk		Last Laughs	They Said What?	Overheard
Fashion criticism	Fashion Police	Oops, What Were They Thinking?	Fashion Trauma		Worst of the Week

sections, many of which appear in every issue. Sections such as "Diva or Down to Earth," and "Star Shots" document the "everyday" lives of celebrities, while "Up Close" and "Loose Talk" claim to give readers a glimpse of the stars' most personal thoughts and actions. Although the specific contents of these sections change from week to week, their basic structure remains the same. Even the names of these categories vary only slightly – the fashion comparison, called "Who Wore It Better?" at *In Touch* and *OK!*, is entitled "Who Wears It Best?" at *Life & Style*. The consistency with which content is presented allows the reader to instantly recognize magazines that belong to the celebrity gossip genre and to predict the type of reading experience she will have.

These themed sections are not the only aspects of the genre's contents that are predetermined; the "editorial focus" of many issues is decided upon more than a year in advance. Each publication maintains an editorial calendar, a chronological schema of the year, which assigns content to issues in anticipation of pre-selected events, holidays, and topics. Table 2.2 culls information from the 2010 editorial calendars

Table 2.2 2010 Editorial calendar

Month	Editorial focus
January	Diets, People's Choice Awards
February	Valentine's Special, Golden Globes, Sundance, Grammy Awards
March	New York Fashion Week, Spring Fashion, Academy Awards
April	Earth Day/Green Issue, Kid's Choice Awards
May	Mother's Day/Celebrity Moms, Cannes Film Festival, Wedding Dresses
June	Father's Day, Swimwear/Hot Bodies
July	Summer Hair/Fashion/Beauty
August	Back to School
September	Back to School, Fall Fashion and Beauty
October	Breast Cancer Awareness (Pink Issue), New York Fashion Week
November	Health and Fitness, Winter Beauty
December	Holiday Gift Guide, Year in Review

of *Us Weekly*, *Life & Style*, *In Touch*, and *Star*; the themes listed in this table represent topics that were covered by two or more publications in a given month.[7] Just as their weekly themed sections mirror one another, the editorial calendars of these publications also reflect a high level of consistency.

Once again, we see that the magazines rely on a series of codes that work to make the text accessible and communicative to the model reader. The predictability and accessibility of the celebrity gossip genre is essential because these characteristics produce the magazines as *readable* texts. The fact that these publications are easy to read is an effect of the consistency with which textual codes are employed throughout the genre.

Nowhere is the consistency of the celebrity gossip brand more apparent than on the magazines' covers. Because the cover is, according to magazine scholar Ellen McCracken, an advertisement for the magazine itself, it must convey critical information about the issue's contents, attract the desired reader, and encourage potential consumers to become interested in the narrative world of the magazine, so much so that they will ultimately purchase that issue (1993: 13–14). "The difference between an OK-selling cover and a great cover is," as *Brandweek*'s Judith Newman points out, "about half a million dollars. In one week."[8] A great deal of time and attention is, therefore, devoted to perfecting the front page. Lauren explains that, at *Us*, editor-in-chief Michael Steele and owner Jann Wenner spend late Monday nights making last-minute decisions about which stories and photographs will make the cover. Everything from the choice of photo and color to the placement of headlines is meticulously considered to not only capture reader attention, but also to maintain the brand identity of the magazine.

The cover establishes the character of the publication; it conveys information about the magazine's readership and positions the magazine in relationship to other products in the market. Therefore, although cover design works to set each issue apart from its competition, it also embraces specific industry norms, lest it be rendered unrecognizable to potential buyers. In order for a front page to be successful, it must not only stand out but blend in. It must be exciting but not deviant, lest it confuse readers who are familiar with the visual standards of the genre.

Thus, regardless of the week's lead story, cover designers are wedded to a specific aesthetic. This aesthetic is established through the use of visual and rhetorical cues which appear throughout the magazines, but which are especially prominent on the covers. Eye-catching graphics, bright colors, and large photographs of female celebrities are often accompanied by bubbles, boxes, and arrows, which draw the potential buyer's eye to key pieces of narrative information. Headlines are bold, bright, and brief. Celebrities are referred to by their first names.

The cacophony of visual information on the celebrity gossip cover is organized so as to ensure that readers will be able to quickly and easily interpret the headlines at a newsstand. Typically, one lead story occupies the center of the cover, articulated through bold-font headlines and large photographs of the celebrities involved. The lead story is flocked by secondary features, which occupy the periphery of the page and are arranged in smaller boxes. Within each box, headlines and photographs inform readers about these secondary narratives. The size and location of content on the gossip magazine cover work to rank the issue's stories, providing readers with visual cues that mark some narratives as noteworthy and others as "shocking," "groundbreaking," or otherwise paramount.

One of the primary ways in which the magazines communicate is through photographs. Images of women are prominently featured throughout, their faces displayed in large, glossy photos. These photos inform the reader that the genre's narratives are about female life, told from a female perspective. For example, the cover of a March 2009 issue of *OK!* features pictures of four smiling stars, three of whom are allegedly pregnant, one who has dropped two dress sizes. Meanwhile, a small photo of a nervous, frightened Jade Goody appears in the upper-right-hand corner. Jade, a reality star who was suffering from terminal cancer during the time of this report, appears tense, her hands folded as if in prayer. Similarly, a large photo of a haggard-looking Kate Middleton dominates the cover of a January 2013 issue of *Star*; the headline blares "New Fears for Kate!" To the left, smaller stories tell of Demi (Moore)'s "wild" trip to Mexico and give a sneak peek at the "Top 10 Hollywood Homewreckers," all of whom are women. These types of images work to establish the celebrity gossip genre as an arena in which female experience and female emotion are paramount.

The value of the visual cannot be overstated. Because images make headlines and sell copies, the cost of celebrity photographs has risen to all-time highs in recent years, with single images of the top female stars bringing millions.[9] As *Us Weekly's* former photo director Brittain Stone notes, some female celebrities have become staples of the gossip press thanks to their ability to "give good magazine." Stone argues that Paris Hilton is one such star because "she's always wearing something colorful . . . If you're a magazine, you run colorful pictures, and she just pops on a page."[10] Visual appeal is so crucial that editors will often favor a so-so story about magazine-friendly Hilton over a "newsy" but less colorful story about Angelina Jolie. Lauren explains:

> The "Love Lives" section is much more picture-driven. It has to be light. It has to be pretty. It has to be loving. We can have amazing reporting about Angelina and she hasn't left the house in a month and the last time she did she wore black. Then we're not going to run that story. This section is bright. These pictures are bright.

As Lauren's statement demonstrates, the availability of high-quality, visually appealing imagery is a key factor in determining the viability of a story. A bit of compelling information, without an attractive photo, is simply not marketable in this industry.

It is no coincidence, then, that these magazines, which contain hundreds of images each week, have emerged at a time in which new advances in digital-imaging technology have revolutionized the way in which photographs are created, dispersed, and edited. Powerful digital cameras, high-speed Internet connectivity, and advanced editing software provide today's designers and editors with instant access to thousands of high-quality images and allow them to edit, format, and revise these images at top speed.

The digital revolution of the late twentieth and early twenty-first centuries has been a driving force in the contemporary celebrity industry, allowing visual and textual information to be acquired and disseminated in a flash. Prior to the 1990s, the process of image acquisition and production was a laborious and time-consuming one; today, a New York editor can view images sent from a Los Angeles photographer seconds after they are shot. *Life & Style* senior photo editor Rob DeMarco is familiar with these changes; he has observed them first hand during his 30-plus years in the photo industry, which has included stints at Rupert Murdoch's *New York Post, National Geographic, U.S. News and World Report,* and *Star*:

> Back in the days before digital, it was a lot of work to move photos. There was no way to do it unless you shipped it FedEx or had cars that would deliver stuff from Manhattan . . . Anything that was on the west coast had to be overnighted. Eventually, it got to the point that if you really needed something in an emergency to be wired to you, you *could* go to the AP [Associated Press] office. They'd be able to scan something and send you three separate separations. What came over were flimsy black-and-white prints. They'd be all slightly different in register and one would say cyan, magenta, and yellow, or whatever the hell it was. They were all black and whites and you couldn't tell what it looked like until they scanned it in at the printing plant and then you'd see color. Sometimes they'd even have in the caption "They're wearing a red dress and a yellow hat." You didn't have a lot to work with.
>
> One of the nightmares was the Academy Awards. That was the biggest event of the year . . . After the red-carpet arrivals, the photographer would give his film to a messenger on a motorcycle, who would bring it over to a lab and get it processed. Then the same thing would happen for the backstage and the awards. Then there were the after-parties. We'd have to get the film processed as fast as possible. And then we'd have somebody sitting on a plane editing the film on the red-eye coming back, then going straight to the printing plant and getting it in the magazine. That's the way it used to work. Then everything went digital and it changed everything, and it made it a hell of a lot easier.

Not only has the emergence of digital photography provided celebrity journalists with high-speed access to the latest images from Hollywood, but it has also sparked a digital gold rush in the photojournalism industry. Rob, who worked with approximately 10 photo companies in the 1980s, now receives numerous weekly emails from new agencies attempting to break into the market.

The growing profitability of celebrity photography has not gone unnoticed by an ever-growing army of paparazzi, who provide many of the candid-style shots that fill the gossip magazines' pages each week. Loud, unrelenting, and in-your-face, paparazzi photographers are known for their unwavering commitment to snapping the most unexpected, most revealing, and most unflattering photos of the rich and famous.

During the 1960s, the Italian director Federico Fellini coined the term "paparazzo" when he gave the name, which roughly translates to "the noise of a buzzing mosquito," to a frenetic, fictional photographer in his film *La Dolce Vita*. During this era, Italian photographers combed the luxurious Via Veneto in hopes of snapping a shot of the wealthy film stars who frequented the area's bars and restaurants. In the 1970s, American photographers like Ron Galella became famous in their own right for capturing elusive images of mega-stars like Jacqueline Kennedy Onassis and Elizabeth Taylor (Howe, 2005).

Today, high-powered, lightweight lenses and digital technologies have allowed the paparazzi to follow closer, shoot faster, and earn more, transforming a small, competitive niche into a booming, cut-throat industry. Eager photographers have been known to go to extreme measures, scaling walls and wrestling bodyguards, in order to capture, and cash in on, newsworthy images. In recent years, their relentless pursuits have earned them the nickname "the stalkerazzi" and their tactics have sparked fervor amongst critics, particularly after Princess Diana's untimely death during an automobile accident that many blamed on relentless photographers. Nevertheless, editors continue to rely on unique and exciting paparazzi shots to reinforce source reporting, enhance the visual appeal of their magazines, and attract reader attention.

Photo editors at celebrity magazines, once eagerly awaiting a handful of shots flown in from LA, are now faced with the daunting task of sorting through 85–90,000 images per day. At *Life & Style*, images are sent, via FTP (file transfer protocol) from photo agencies to a digital server called

MediaGrid. Editors then look at thousands of images, 99 percent of which, according to Rob's former colleague Susanne, "nobody really wants to see," in hopes of finding the week's most desirable photos. The sheer volume of available content makes the editing process tedious and time-consuming. When an image finally makes it into the magazine, editors like Rob, whose relentless search is often interrupted by phone calls and emails from agencies and paparazzi, feel the finished product is nothing short of a "miracle."

But in spite of all this, images are, in many ways, the core of the celebrity gossip genre. "There are a lot of good pictures of Kate Hudson with this guy that she's co-starring with," says Rob of an intriguing set of photographs that he recently reviewed at *Life & Style*. "They're on the beach, frolicking, and they're kissing and having a good time. You get photos like that and they can run a whole page, a whole spread . . . You get a good set of pictures, that's a story in itself." Who can forget the photographs of Britney Spears driving through LA, her unbuckled, infant son atop her lap? Or the first pictures of Ashlee Simpson, post-nose job? For celebrity gossip magazines, the adage "a picture's worth a thousand words" holds true, and photos of famous women are the industry's primary selling point.

Images make the magazines easy to consume – skim, scan, and flip through. Bonnie Fuller, the editor who helped transform *Us* and *Star* into industry leaders, has been accused of building her career on the mantra "Nobody likes to read"; the magazines often reflect this paradigm, their colorful images and bite-sized captions provide for a reading experience that is easily enjoyable.[11] Indeed, audiences often engage them without actually reading much at all. "We always joke," says Lauren, "someone spent an entire day writing this. You don't read any of it. You're looking at the photos and then you're done. People don't read what we write."

The magazines provide maximum information with minimal text. Dozens of large, glossy photographs enhance narrative impact and accessibility while allowing readers to become quickly immersed in the celebrity story world. "You sit in the subway and you watch somebody read the magazine and it's a story that you spent six hours composing and they literally read the captions, look at the pictures, and do this [flips the pages]." But Lauren does not consider this type of reading a bad thing. The magazines "take twenty minutes to read and it's twenty minutes when you're having 'me time.' We definitely craft [the magazine] to be that part of your week that's for you." Sarah agrees, noting that many readers enjoy the magazines while getting a manicure or relaxing on the beach. Like a trip to the salon, the magazines are designed to provide a break from the everyday, a way of taking time out to care for one's self.[12] By creating a reading experience that is predictable and accessible, celebrity journalists ensure that their readers' "me time" will be an enjoyable escape.

But these images are not only used as attention-grabbers. They are also a key strategy for hailing the genre's core readership. The photos featured in celebrity weeklies are not of just any women, but of famous females who are demographically similar to the genre's model reader. A content analysis of 39 magazine covers published between November and December 2009 shows that female celebrities between the ages of 29 and 32 appear most frequently, and 81.75 percent of the women depicted were between the ages of 18 and 34. By prominently featuring celebrities who are the same age as their model reader, editors inform that reader that the magazine is "for her."

Further, these images encourage readers to identify with celebrity women. Scholarship in the field of audience studies suggests that identification occurs when audiences recognize

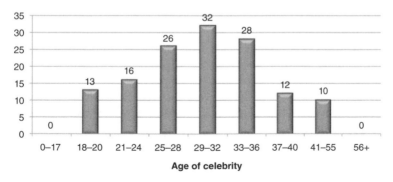

Figure 2.2 Frequency of celebrity appearance by age, November–December 2009[13]

themselves in and adopt the thoughts, goals, or emotions of particular characters, in this case celebrities (Cohen, 2001; Green, Brock, and Kaufman, 2004). Images of famous women encourage female readers to identify with and participate in gossip narratives. In addition, a particular type of identification, similarity identification, occurs when audiences recognize that they share one or more characteristics with a particular figure and therefore feel a sense of affinity (Feilitzen and Linne, 1975). When readers experience similarity identification, they may recognize themselves and their own emotions in their celebrity counterparts; this identification is, as we will see in chapter 3, a key element of reader enjoyment.

Like photos, color is also used to emphasize the feminine nature of the celebrity gossip genre. "There's a color palette that our design team works with," says Lauren of the vivid shades that brighten *Us Weekly*'s front page. "Our art department and our art directors are very mindful of the different color combinations. You're pretty much only ever going to see blue, yellow, pink, green on our cover. Lots of yellow, lots of pink." *Us* is not the only magazine with this aesthetic; all celebrity weeklies use hot pinks, canary yellows, and bright blues, enhancing the genre's playful, upbeat persona. These colors work to further gender the genre since, unlike men's magazines, which rely heavily on primary colors, grays, and black, women's magazines often feature saturated brights: neon pinks, blues, greens, and yellows (King, 2001). Coupled with photographs of female celebs, this specific color palette works to visually alert potential readers to the feminine focus of the genre.

In addition, images are often color-coded so that particular hues become explanatory mechanisms through which narrative intricacies are made visually apparent. As Judith Williamson argues in her analysis of visual meaning-making, color serves as an important communicative tool, linking people, objects, and ideas and creating a narrative structure through these linkages (1978: 20–5).

An example of this type of color-coding can be seen on the November 2009 cover of *Us Weekly*, whose headline proclaims "Fergie Betrayed." A large image of pop singer Fergie and her husband, actor Josh Duhamel, spans the cover.

A smaller, inset photo in the lower-right-hand corner shows a blonde woman wearing a blue and white bikini, seated provocatively on a bed. The *Us* logo is bright yellow, mirroring the canary-yellow dress worn by Fergie. Meanwhile, a hot-pink box, directly situated between Fergie and Josh's faces, cries "Cheating Shock"; another box, the same shade of pink, hangs above the photo of the woman in a bikini, identifying her as "The Stripper." The blaring pink alerts readers to Josh's alleged misdeeds, visually connecting the image of "The Stripper" to the horror of the "Cheating Shock." Not only does color help to establish a narrative arc, but it also works to emotionally position the reader in relationship to the story. Dressed in black, Josh appears guilty and sullen, his eyes averted from the camera. In sharp contrast to her husband, Fergie's eye contact connects her with the reader; her shocking-yellow dress visually links the singer with the magazine's logo, thus identifying her as one of "us" and encouraging readers to position themselves as Fergie supporters before ever reading the story.

Here, we see the color yellow used to code the model reader as one of "us," an individual who is aligned both with Fergie and with the magazine itself. We also see how the genre uses personal pronouns to directly address its audience. "I," "you," "we," and "us" – these words do not only imply a model reader, but directly hail that reader, rhetorically insinuating her into the narrative of the gossip story. These

Figure 2.3 *Us Weekly*, November 16, 2009. Courtesy of Wenner Media. All rights reserved. Reprinted by permission

personal pronouns are a staple of the genre, used throughout the magazines to continuously stitch the audience into the narrative. As they hail the model reader, these pronouns also work to once again gender that reader as female. When *Life & Style* proclaims, "I want those shoes for less," for example, the shoes that are desired are women's shoes; the implied "I," therefore, is a female "I."[14] In this way, the magazines actively and purposefully engage their model reader in a conversation that is about women, between women.

The use of personal pronouns also establishes a direct connection with the model reader; words such as *you* and *us* imply an interaction between text and audience while positioning the magazine as a guide to the celebrity world. This intimate, chatty tone invites readers to think of the magazine as a gossipy friend and personal guide (Douglas, 2010). Further, these pronouns link readers to what Joke Hermes calls an "extended family" (1995). The repertoire of the extended family, explains Hermes, "engenders a highly personal form of address in which solidarity and connectedness resound . . . [It] simply draws a wide circle of people into a person's private life by discussing them intimately. On an imaginary level, this creates a form of community" (1995: 298, 302). Celebrity gossip magazines address their readers as members of an extended family, hailing them as participants in a larger, imagined group of gossipers and gossipees.

The extended-family repertoire is further emphasized through one of the genre's hallmark visual techniques: arrows. These brightly colored pointers, superimposed over specific areas of visual interest, serve as an explanatory mechanism, drawing attention to and providing a visual commentary on key elements of the narrative while establishing the editorial point of view. For example, an October 2009 cover of *OK!* features a lead story that alleges Jennifer Aniston is "Pregnant at 40!" A large photo of a smiling Aniston fills the center of the page; meanwhile, to the left, a smaller inset photo of the actress, clad in a form-fitting silver dress, has been adorned with a bright yellow arrow, pointing to her midsection. The text beside the arrow reads "It's a bump!" The arrow supposedly confirms Jen's pregnancy by alerting any readers who might have missed it to the visual "proof" of the "bump."[15] Here, we see how arrows literally point out important narrative details to the reader. These visual cues place the magazine in direct conversation with that reader, gesturing, as a friend would, showing her where to look.

But if the genre uses these types of cues to imply a dialogue between magazine and reader, it also works to create a sense of conversation between readers and celebrities. *Us Weekly* features an interview entitled "25 Things You Don't Know About Me." In it (usually female) celebrities divulge personal information about themselves: their favorite colors, meals, books, and pastimes. The entire interview is told in the first person, from the star's point of view. In an April 2013 issue, for example, reality television star Nene Leakes confides in readers, "I have a shy side" and "My celebrity crush is Simon Cowell." Through this trademark style of direct address, with its emphasis on the personal divulging of secrets, celebrities and readers are linked in an extended family of females.

In the third and final part of the triad, these rhetorical cues place readers in conversation with one another, inviting them to imagine the responses of fellow (unknown) audience members. This mediated reader-to-reader interaction is most clearly encouraged through interactive polls and questionnaires. For example, the "Who Wore It Best?" poll (a version of which appears in every publication) presents photographs of celebrities wearing similar outfits, and invites readers to judge the subtle differences between images in order to decide which celebrity "wore it best." At *Us Weekly*, *OK!*, and *Life & Style*, these images are coupled with the results of a public poll – as former *Us Weekly* intern Joy Wood explains, magazine staff ask 100 people in Times Square or Rockefeller Center to rate images of famous women. The celebrity who receives the majority of the votes is deemed the winner. In this way, interactive polls work to establish a sense of connection and camaraderie between an imagined family of readers.

Nowhere does the discursive construction of these familial bonds appear more clearly than in the letter I received in the spring of 2010 as my subscription to *Us Weekly* neared its expiration. The envelope, which was sealed with a magenta "kiss," read "We're about to BREAK UP!" Once opened, the letter contained an "anti-break-up form," which urged me not to "let us come to an end" and pleaded, "We need to hear from you right away" – "Don't keep us waiting." The yellow and pink flyer featured a superimposed "tear" down the center of the page, with pink text confirming "The Split." Through its graphic symbolism, the anti-break-up form reinforces the message that by ending my subscription, I would not merely be discontinuing my purchase of a weekly gossip magazine, but would, in fact, be severing my relationship with "us" and rescinding my membership in the gossip family.

The celebrity gossip magazine, therefore, not only produces itself for a single model reader, but for an entire cohort of readers. It hails those readers simultaneously, inviting them to participate in an extended family that is created and sustained through the text. This imagined network is, crucially, a female one – both the celebrities and the readers who participate in it are women. In this way, celebrity gossip magazines offer their readers the opportunity to feel connected to millions of women, both known and unknown, famous and ordinary. This sense of connection is one of the primary affordances of the genre. Women's magazines, writes media critic Naomi Wolf, "offer an electrifying feeling that women are too seldom granted, though men in their groups feel it continually, of being plugged in without hostility to a million like-minded people of the same sex" (1992: 76).[16] As we will see in the following chapters, readers take pleasure in connecting with and relating to other women vis-à-vis the contents of the magazines. The fact that the celebrity gossip genre offers its readers this opportunity for connection is not a happy accident, but rather the result of strategic choices made by writers, editors, designers, and publishers who strive to appeal to their target audience.

But it is not only the female-focused content or the easy-to-read stories that attract readers – famous females also play a key role As the magazines show Miley walking her dog, Ke$ha slurping a Starbucks, and Gwyneth playing at the park, they invite us to imagine our own experiences, to relate *our* pets, *our* lattes, and *our* playground follies to those of famous women who are, the magazines insist, "just like us." And so female celebrities become part of our extended family not only by virtue of their age and gender, but because their experiences are presented as typical, understandable, and shared. The link between reader and celebrity (and between reader and text) is therefore reliant on a powerful motif that has come to dominate the contemporary cultural landscape in the United States. Here and now, celebrities are no longer held at a distance. They peer out at us from our televisions and laptop screens. They wave at us from the red carpet. They tweet to us. Once our idols, the stars are now our friends. Celebrities have become ordinary.

3
Stars on Earth
The Paradox of Ordinary Celebrity

The November 2010 cover of *W Magazine*, designed by conceptual artist Barbara Kruger, features a photo of Kim Kardashian, nude, hands on hips, covered only by three red strips that read "It's all about me/I mean you/I mean me." In the accompanying article, Kardashian explains how she manages her business ventures – her website, boutiques, perfume brands (she even has a line of designer lollipops) – all the while emphasizing her close relationship with her fans, whom she views as sisters and friends. Indeed, Kardashian has built a business empire on her ability to present herself as a kind of everywoman (she is, as writer Lynn Hirschberg points out, "the star of a reality show . . . which means she's famous for being herself") (2010: 110). Kardashian's success is indicative of our contemporary celebrity culture, which applauds stars not for their outstanding talent or honorable achievements, but for their ability to be "down to earth." Today's celebrities are human – no longer idols, they are now our friends. Gossip magazines are part of a growing celebrity industry – which also includes talk shows, reality television programs, and blogs – that has succeeded by insisting to audiences that celebrities are ordinary people. But why has this approach to fame been so successful? Surely it has allowed Kardashian and others to enhance their stardom and grow their bank accounts, but is the motif of the ordinary celebrity really all about them, or is it also about us?

Fame has always been a bundle of contradictions, requiring those who possess it to occupy a curious middle ground between the exceptional and the commonplace. According to Leo Braudy, who traces the historical roots of fame in his book *The Frenzy of Renown*, the idea that "a famous person has to be a socially acceptable individualist, different enough to be interesting, yet similar enough not to be threatening or destructive" has existed for centuries (1986: 8). This was as true for Caesar and Prince Albert as it is for Madonna. Throughout history, well-known figures have intentionally shaped their image so as not to appear very different from their public. In the mid-nineteenth century, for example, Napoleon III and Queen Victoria distributed photographs of themselves wearing everyday clothing as a way of re-presenting themselves as middle class and, therefore, less distant from their subjects (Hamilton and Hargreaves, 2001: 13). Their actions point to the paradox of the ordinary celebrity.

Over the course of the twentieth century, the ordinariness of celebrities has been amplified thanks, in large part, to technological innovations. Photography, for example, has played a crucial role in the construction of fame since its invention in the 1830s. The mass distribution of images transformed public figures into famous faces, recognizable to the public. By the early 1900s, advances in cinematography allowed film-makers such as D. W. Griffith to employ "close-up" shots, providing cinema-goers with an unprecedented view of the movie star and thereby facilitating an intimate encounter between the two, all the while enhancing the star's aura (Walker, 1970: 21). Fan magazines of the 1920s and 1930s reflected these developments, providing readers with large, tightly cropped images of well-known actors and actresses. Meanwhile, the new medium of radio furthered the sense of connection between public figures and private individuals; listeners at the time reported feeling as though the popular singers of the day were speaking directly "to them" (Merton and Lowenthal, 1946). But perhaps the greatest change in the relationship between audience and celebrity can be traced to the 1950s, as television beamed the faces and voices of actors and actresses into the living rooms, and daily lives, of millions of Americans. The domestic nature of television viewing created a sense of intimacy and familiarity between actor and viewer, which worked to dilute the star's aura, making her ever more accessible (Marshall 1997: 119–22).

If early television helped to break the celebrity image, in recent years, the emergence of reality television shows, social media, and participatory websites, particularly Facebook and YouTube, have shattered it. "Whole media formats are now devoted to, and the contemporary media consumer has become increasingly accustomed to, following what happens to the 'ordinary' person who has been plucked from obscurity to enjoy a highly circumscribed celebrity," argues Graeme Turner, who calls this shift the demotic turn (2010: 12). Demotic media (DIY-websites, talk shows, and reality television) emphasize the everyday event, the could-be-anyone individual. The popularity of these formats has, since the 1980s, led to the proliferation of "ordinary celebrities" – the cheerleader turned model, the part-time blogger turned journalist, the family dog turned YouTube sensation. Today, even traditional stars – actors, musicians, and politicians – are increasingly portrayed as "normal," everyday people. Contemporary celebrity magazines reflect the demotic turn; indeed, the ordinary celebrity is one of the genre's trademarks. But has celebrity *really* been democratized? Or have contemporary stars, like their historical counterparts, simply discovered a new strategy for enhancing their fame in a media landscape where the line between star and audience is ever thinning?

The Ordinary Celebrity

Realness and authenticity carry much weight in celebrity media. As celebrity scholar Su Holmes notes, "The illusion of access and intimacy remains the dominant structuring force in celebrity texts" (2006: 54). Even for savvy fans, the celebrity's perceived authenticity remains an essential component of enjoyment; therefore, stars must appear authentic and "real" in order to appeal to fans and remain popular. For this reason, Joshua Gamson argues, "the question of who and what celebrities really are must be answerable" (1994:

171). In recent years, celebrities have employed the motif of the ordinary to exert control over how the question of self is answered. *Who am I?* The stars simply reply, *"I am just like you. I am ordinary and therefore you already know the real me."*

Increasingly, celebrities have taken an active role in the construction and maintenance of their public persona; they hire publicists, agents, stylists, personal attendants – a veritable army of helpers – to assist them in maintaining an "ordinary" image (Gamson, 1994). In the contemporary marketplace, one of the key sites of image production is the celebrity gossip press. For this reason, many stars have become active participants in the production of gossip narratives, providing journalists with carefully choreographed information about themselves. According to magazine editors, celebrities often relay "private" information or official comments to journalists via their handlers, publicists, and managers. Lauren Schutte explains:

> Nine times out of ten, celebrities or those who work directly for them confirm stories before they are sent to the printer. The people who are in this magazine on a weekly basis want to be in this magazine. They may not publicly want to let it be known that they want to be in this magazine, but if you're on a red carpet every night and you're eating out at restaurants in which paparazzi live, you're doing those things because you want to get photographed. And if you want to get photographed it's because you want to be in here. . . . We'll have people call and basically say, "What do I need to do to become interesting to you? Do you want a baby? Do I need to get married?"

Like Lauren, photo editor Rob DeMarco (who describes celebrities as "complete publicity hounds") argues that the stars are active participants in the creation of celebrity gossip. "You see the same people over and over and over again. If I see another picture of Audrina [Patridge] walking out of Starbucks with a cup of coffee I'm gonna scream," says Rob, who like Lauren, contends that stars who make themselves available to the press are intentionally courting media attention in order to enhance their public profile.

According to celebrity journalists, much of what appears in gossip magazines is carefully controlled by celebrities and their teams, who strategically tailor their behavior in order to bolster their persona or to draw attention to their latest film or television show. And while some stars may try to avoid the paparazzi and the gossip press, others take advantage of it. In a 2007 interview with LX TV, then-editor-in-chief of *Us Weekly*, Janice Min, had this to say about the relationship between celebrities and the media:

> Does the media get invasive in celebrities' private lives? Yes, they do. Do celebrities go along with it and often offer up information and access and play an active role in their own media? Absolutely. . . . Let's not forget also, when you're a celebrity, you're not in a race to cure cancer, you're in a race to be publicized. If you're a celebrity, you cease to exist if your photo isn't in *Us Weekly*. You cease to exist if no one is talking about you. And that's the end of your livelihood. That's it. So with celebrities it's part of the game to say you don't like so much attention and it's definitely a bigger part of the game to seek the attention.

In a media landscape that is saturated with information and fascinated by the ordinary, celebrities have increasingly begun to develop innovative strategies for attracting media attention. Rob explains:

> One of the things is that at the Halloween time of the year, the people want to make sure they get their pictures taken with their kids. They all show up at this particular farmer's market in LA that sells pumpkins and they have a slide. It's like a photo op. They know they're going to get photographed. They don't try to dodge it at all. Sometimes they tip certain paparazzi in advance that they're going to be there. This is strictly for a setup so that they get their pictures in the paper. They dress up nicely and the kids are there. They actually try to look informal but it's very, very posed.
>
> So it's photo ops that are basically set up by the celebrities. They go to parks. They do the same thing, pushing the kids on swings. Some celebrities, they walk their dog every day at the same time of the day. And many, many of them do tip the paparazzi in advance. Like, "I'm going to be over at a certain store tomorrow if you want to get pictures." Or they have their people tip them. So there's tons of cooperation. You can even tell by the type of shots that we get. They almost look like they're set up.

There are certain celebrities that actually contract paparazzi or photo agencies to set up shoots. They might do shots on the beach, they might do loving couple shots, things of that nature. In which case, many times, they get a cut of the money for what the pictures sold for. So they're even in on it from a monetary standpoint sometimes.

Also, if a certain tabloid runs a story that the [stars] find to be negative like, "We haven't seen these two together in three weeks. Are they having marital problems?", the next day they'll be out on the street posing together to try to make that story look fake. Even if it's right, they want to control the publicity the way *they* want to control it. They try to diffuse certain stories by photo ops and that, many times, is very contrived as well. Celebrities work with the system to get pictures in [the magazines] on a daily basis. Let there be no mistake.

Rob's comments not only reveal celebrities' willingness to work with the tabloid press, but also show how "ordinary" life is, for the stars, a bargaining chip that can be used to gain publicity and control one's public image. The "genuineness" of the star is not only a tool for boosting her symbolic power, but also for enhancing her economic value, for it is through the performance of authenticity that celebrities bolster their appeal and thereby strengthen their ability to sell themselves and their brand.[1]

Adrienne Lai, whose research examines the role of authenticity in celebrity photography, writes that celebrities' willingness to participate in "the economy of tabloid images" speaks to "the currency of the real" (2006: 220). Because audience enjoyment depends upon the star's ability to appear authentic, celebrities must seem sincere, genuine, and "real" in order to remain in the good graces of the press and the public (Gamson, 1994). Sincerity, genuineness, and reality are, however, slippery concepts; therefore, celebrities must develop concrete strategies that will effectively convey these traits. The trope of the ordinary provides a solution to the question of authenticity (Holmes, 2006). An individual who is genuine and down to earth does not have a chef, a driver, or a maid; she cooks her own dinner, hauls herself around town, cleans her own bathroom. A celebrity whose life is defined by the banal and the everyday, a celebrity who is ordinary, is, therefore authentic.

Still, the notion of the ordinary celebrity remains a paradoxical one because the lives of the stars are, by definition, exceptional (Dyer, 1998; Ellis, 2000). How can celebrities, who are, in reality, very different from their fans, present themselves as pedestrian? The solution lies in the realm of private life. As Rob describes, certain celebrities strategically provide the press with photographs and information about their "private" lives so as to appear ordinary. Rob's account, however, makes clear the fact that the everyday lives of stars are, in actuality, far from ordinary and anything but private.

One celebrity who has built her brand and career on a careful, public performance of private life is Paris Hilton. Every aspect of Hilton's personal life – from her pet chihuahua, to her favorite catchphrases, to, some speculate, her sex tape – are a part of the heiress's image. In the documentary film *Paris Hilton Inc.* (2007, CBC Television), film-makers show how Paris provides the press with an itinerary of her comings and goings, and explain how the socialite changes outfits between each activity in hopes that photographers and magazines will more readily print multiple images of her if she is wearing different attire.[2] Hilton's acute awareness of how she will be portrayed in the media and the elaborate steps that she takes to provide the press with a choreographed version of her daily activities points to the way in which, for some stars, "private life" is a complex performance designed to promote and manage the celebrity brand.

For stars like Hilton, the relationship between private life and public persona has been transformed into what Joshua Meyrowitz calls a middle region or side-stage performance (1985). Meyrowitz's side stage emerges from the theory of interpersonal communication developed by sociologist Erving Goffman. In his 1959 book, *The Presentation of Self in Everyday Life*, Goffman argues that individuals actively work to produce a desirable public self, which operates on the front stage, while concealing their hidden, inner workings back stage, behind the scenes. According to Goffman, all people, famous or not, engage in a process of frontstage management, carefully presenting themselves in particular ways so as to mitigate the complexities of social relations. While the front stage functions as a public performance of our self as we wish others to see it, the back stage is a private self, a self that is only known to a select few. In contemporary celebrity culture, however, the dividing line between front and back stage has become increasingly blurred. What was once back stage is no longer a private space, but a supplemental performance area or side stage in which "private life" is publicly enacted.

On this side stage, celebrities and their teams are now involved in what Gamson calls the process of fabrication (the fictional creation of images, stories, and personas) and blurring (the molding, manipulation, and management of these images, stories, and personas), strategies which allow stars to appear ordinary and authentic while also retaining control over their public image (1994: 172). Thus, while celebrity journalism claims to throw open the curtains, bring up the house lights, and give audiences a peek into the private, backstage lives of the stars, the back stage is now, in actuality, a supplemental performance area, increasingly monitored and managed by the celebrities themselves. Side-stage performances of ordinary life afford celebrities the opportunity to control their image and enhance their authenticity and so this apparent willingness of the star to be just like the rest of us, this "warts-and-all authenticity" is, in reality, "a strategy to propel [the star] to great celebrification, far, far away from such ordinariness" (Redmond, 2006: 28).

Between You and Me: The Magazine as Mediator

Celebrity gossip magazines provide stars with a forum in which to perform their "ordinariness." They do not do so as a favor to celebrities, but as a way of ensuring their own success. The genre claims to give readers the opportunity to know the stars as they "really" are, to afford them access to "the truth and the inside scoop about celebrities."[3] In order to fulfill this promise, however, there must be a real, authentic star that is available to be known. This poses a problem for the magazines because, as we have seen, celebrity is a complicated chimera, a blend of fact and fiction, reality and performance, back- and front-stage work. To provide readers with access to the "real" star is not to simply report on a person as she actually exists, but to create a version of that person that appeals to a particular audience. Therefore, in order to afford readers access to the authentic celebrity, the magazines must first construct a version of celebrity that appears real. To accomplish this, the genre draws upon the motif of the ordinary celebrity because the ordinary, everyday, is a useful, tangible heuristic for authenticity. By presenting celebrities as ordinary people, the magazines not only create the "real," "authentic" star, but also establish themselves as gatekeepers through whom access to that star becomes possible. In claiming to give readers access to the ordinary lives of celebrities, the magazines position themselves as know-it-all friends, gossipy insiders, and indispensable guides.

The production of the ordinary celebrity is most apparent in one of the genre's trademark features, the "Just Like Us" photo montage. Consisting of candid photographs of celebrities engaging in humdrum activities – eating lunch, grocery shopping, or playing with their children – these images provide readers with visual evidence of the stars' alleged normalcy. At *Us*, it is called, "Stars – They're Just Like Us!," at *Star*, "Are They Normal or Not?," and at *Life & Style*, "Diva or Down to Earth?" but whatever the title, these sections all reinforce the idea that celebrities are ordinary people. In some magazines, this section also contains photos of stars acting *abnormally* – wearing kooky costumes, eating bizarre foods, or interacting with strange animals. Within this editorial framework, however, depictions of celebrities behaving in abnormal ways – as *not* normal or as "divas" – further reinforces the idea that stars *should* be ordinary. The "Just Like Us" photo montage epitomizes the ordinary celebrity ideal and clearly illustrates the way in which celebrity gossip magazines are invested in and actively work to construct this motif.

While "Just Like Us" photos explicitly mark celebrities as "normal," the construction of the ordinary celebrity is not limited to this particular section, but rather occurs throughout the magazines. Celebrity weeklies use a variety of visual and linguistic cues to remind readers that stars are "just like them." One of the cheekiest ways in which the genre achieves

Figure 3.1 *Star*, December 14, 2009, p. 4. Courtesy of American Media, Inc. All rights reserved. Reprinted by permission / *Us Weekly*, November 5, 2012, p. 26. Courtesy of Wenner Media. All rights reserved. Reprinted by permission

this is by depicting celebrities reading the very magazines in which they are featured. A December 14, 2009, issue of *Star*, for example, features a photograph of *Gossip Girl* actress Kelly Rutherford pushing her daughter, Helena, in a stroller. Poking out from over the top of her basket is a copy of *Star*; a giant white arrow emphasizes the presence of the magazine while an enlarged, inset image of the issue leaves readers with no doubt that, like them, Kelly Rutherford reads *Star*. Similarly, a November 5, 2012, issue of *Us Weekly* shows actress Krysten Ritter perusing the latest issue of the magazine. These types of star-as-reader images work to erase the boundary between actor and audience. If stars read the magazines, so the logic goes, then they are no different from you, dear reader, who are, at this very moment, reading the magazine. In this way, star-as-reader images emphasize the ordinariness of celebrities, furthering the notion that they are "just like us," while reinforcing the status of the magazine itself.

The similarity between celebrity and reader is further emphasized by the organization of advertisements within the magazines. Editorial features are often juxtaposed with ads whose products match or mirror the corresponding narrative. Typically, the left page contains celebrity stories while the right page contains a related advertisement. When the reader opens to that spread, she will encounter this carefully paired content. For example, an October 2009 issue of *Us Weekly* featured a story about "Hollywood's Hottest Hounds," in which images and captions describe celebrities' relationships with their pets. This story was paired with an advertisement for 9 Lives cat food. Similarly, an issue of *Life & Style* from that same month reported that leggings were a new trend for fall, and featured photographs of celebrities sporting the style – the opposite page contained an advertisement for Fila athletic wear, the model donning black leggings similar to those worn by the stars on the opposite page.

Not only are these juxtapositions a clever advertising strategy, but they also work to imply a direct relationship between reader and star that is based upon an ethos of consumption. The "Hollywood Hound" story, for example, invites readers to imagine the relationship that celebrities have with their pets; they walk their dogs, play with them, and, like all pet owners, feed them. In this way, the strategic placement of advertising and editorial content encourages readers to feel that they are engaged in consumption practices that are similar to those of famous women. Halle Berry feeds her pet, just like I do. Nicky Hilton buys leggings and so might I. Through these implied similarities, the magazines cast celebrities and readers as doppelgängers, individuals who share common life experiences. The choice and placement of advertisements works to construct a metanarrative, reinforcing "ordinary" celebrities' perceived similarity to readers and further encouraging identification.

In addition to these visual techniques, the magazines also use linguistic cues. The most notable of these is the repetition of first names – Jen, Jessica, Britney, and Katie. Within the genre, this simple yet powerful technique hails both readers and stars as participants in an ongoing conversation; last names need not be included because, the magazine implies, readers are already familiar with these women. Thus, the use of first names implies a relationship between star and reader that pre-dates the reader's engagement with any particular issue of the magazine. As media critic Susan Douglas argues, "calling them by their first names or nicknames, addressing them in such a personal fashion . . . the strategy is to cultivate the notion that we have an ongoing relationship with these stars, that we are in on their lives and thus should engage with them pretty much the same way we do with people we know" (2010: 248). The ordinary celebrity is always already known by the reader and this knowability, as we shall see, is a crucial feature of audience enjoyment. Furthermore, because surnames are often used as a sign of respect and deference, the fact that readers and celebs are on a first-name-only basis suggests that theirs is a relationship between equals and friends. This implied relationship is emphasized by the use of personal pronouns. On the cover of an October 5, 2009, issue of *Life & Style*, for example, Khloe (Kardashian) gushes, "I'm so in love," while Jen (Aniston) proclaims, "I want a baby now!" Here, direct quotations and the word "I" are used to convey the celebrity's point of view, while implying an ongoing, personal conversation between reader and star. But let us not forget, this dialogue is possible only through the magazine – established as a gossipy, mutual friend who facilitates the relationship between star and audience.

Despite their insistence that the stars are "just like us," celebrity gossip magazines do at times stray from the motif of the ordinary celebrity, drawing readers' attention to the "fabulous" and "glamorous" aspects of celebrity life. Such narratives often emphasize the stars' wealth, illustrating their spending habits in great detail. This conspicuous consumption, however, is coupled with articles containing strategies for readers hoping to model the lifestyle of their favorite stars, on a budget. A December 2009 issue of *Life & Style*, for instance, instructs readers on how to achieve "Star Style For Less." The article, which quips "These Finds Only Look Expensive," compares the designer fashions worn by famous women with similar items purchased from department stores and bargain retailers. While the article positions famous women as objects of envy, it also works to diminish the economic differences between reader and star by insisting that, regardless of income, all women can, with a bit of savvy, achieve the latest style. These types of articles not only temper the financial disparities between readers and celebrities, but also establish the magazine as a secret-keeper who provides the reader with strategies, solutions, and insider know-how that will allow her to bridge the gap between herself and the star.

While the "look for less" story is a popular staple of the genre, other types of narratives also focus on the financial success of the stars in ways that reinforce the magazines' gatekeeper status. The "tour" narrative, for example, claims to give readers a glimpse into the "real" lives of the stars, literally bringing them inside the world of the rich and famous – their homes and closets, nurseries and pantries. The February 2, 2009, issue of *Star* magazine contains one such tour narrative; in it, an eight-page spread takes readers "inside" "Celebrity Cribs." The story consists primarily of large photographs of living rooms, kitchens, bedrooms, and swimming pools – all looking remarkably well-styled, clean, and devoid of any personal objects – which are coupled with images of the homes' smiling inhabitants.

These "tour" stories often contain photos of the stars posing with their possessions, looking flawless and happy as they show off their material success. While these photos, on the surface, appear quite different from the candid "just like us" shots, both types of images actually serve the same purpose. According to journalism scholar Karin Becker, posed photos of celebrities, like candid shots, suggest to viewers that they are seeing the stars as they "really" are:

> The plain photograph of the person posing at home . . . [is] arranged in the same manner that characterizes the pictures of non-famous people. . . . These people all appear relaxed and happy. The obviously domestic environments naturalize the stars. . . . At the same time, through angle and eye-contact with the camera, they are brought down to the viewer's level. The photographic construction which presents the private person as someone "just like us" accomplishes the same task when framing the public figure. (2008: 89)

In this way, posed photos work to produce the stars as ordinary people, despite their obvious wealth.

These types of tour narratives use captions to further diminish the economic difference between star and audience. While the "Celebrity Cribs" story emphasizes the opulence of the stars' properties, noting their multimillion dollar price tags and luxurious amenities, captions explaining how Ashley Olsen can "whip up feasts for herself" in her kitchen and predicting that Vanessa Hudgens will "enjoy bubble baths galore" in her spa tub insist that celebrities, despite their wealth, are no different from readers. By leading a virtual tour of the stars' "real" lives, the magazines once again cast themselves as knowledgeable guides, gossipy gatekeepers without whom these arenas would remain off limits.

Even those narratives that emphasize the economic differences between celebrities and readers ultimately work to produce the star as ordinary (i.e., real) while establishing the magazine as a critical mediator. The motif of the ordinary celebrity is crucial to the success of the genre, then, because it is through this motif that the magazines produce the celebrity as a knowable entity and are therefore able to fulfill their promise of providing readers access to the star as she really is. In addition, this strategy encourages readers to develop a parasocial relationship with famous women, with whom they can relate and identify. As demonstrated in the previous chapter, celebrity gossip magazines are not entertainment magazines, but women's magazines; their content revolves around topics that matter to women at a particular life stage, topics that are often considered personal in nature. The ordinary celebrity, the celebrity whose "personal" life is made available to the public, therefore speaks directly to the concerns of that readership.

She and I: Audiences and the Ordinary Celebrity

It is all so much the same as it used to be in my young days. *Modern Society* and *Tit Bits* and all the rest of them. A lot of gossip. A lot of scandal. A great preoccupation with who is in love with who, and all the rest of it. Really, you know, practically the same sort of thing that goes on in St. Mary Mead. And in the Development, too. Human nature, I mean, is just the same everywhere.

Jane Marple, as told by Agatha Christie[4]

As we have seen, and following Christie's formulation above, both celebrity gossip magazines and the stars themselves are invested in and benefit from the motif of the ordinary celebrity. But why should readers be concerned with whether the stars are presented as idols or as friends? It is because celebrities as friends, as ordinary people, perform a function that idols cannot – they serve as avatars who publicly enact, and thereby make knowable, women's personal experiences.

The cultural critic Raymond Williams argues that one of the key features of the English novel is its ability to depict people and their relationships in a "knowable" way. According to Williams, the novel does not merely reflect social relations as they exist, but personalizes these relations, articulating them in ways that make them knowable and communicable, thus creating a knowable community (1970). Popular feminine texts have been shown to provide this kind of community for audiences; as Rosalind Coward writes in her analysis of soap opera, "[The characters'] stories are our stories and what happens in their lives must have a resonance in our lives, so that the audience is willing to embrace the drama" (1985: 105). Scholarship has also shown that popular feminine narratives result in audiences using those stories to think about and discuss their own lives (Hobson, 1989; Katz and Liebes, 1990).

Celebrity gossip magazines function thus for contemporary readers. By constructing celebrities as ordinary people, the magazines create a knowable community, which collectivizes and articulates common concerns and anxieties. Celebrities are ideally suited to perform the functions of the knowable community because, in their ubiquity, they are innately knowable, despite the fact that they are not actually known. "If the United States is high school," explains Lauren Schutte, "celebrities are the popular kids. They are who you want to know about, but you already know them." Still, in order to be *knowable*, celebrities must not only be well known, but must also be people whose thoughts, emotions, and experiences are comprehensible because they are not so very different from our own. In other words, stars must appear to be ordinary human beings.

One of the key features of the knowable community is its ability to collectivize elements of the social world by personalizing them, by giving them a face and a name. In their role as ordinary people, celebrities perform precisely this function for female readers. Because the majority of the stars featured in celebrity gossip magazines are around the same age as readers, stories about the ordinary lives of famous women – their personal emotions and experiences – may provide readers with a recognizable manifestation of their own feelings and affairs and, in doing so, allow for moments of identification. "I think people see themselves in celebrities," says *OK!*'s Valerie Nome. "You see Kim Kardashian going through a breakup and you think, 'I went through a breakup,' and what that was like. How did she get over it? What can I apply to my own life?" Celebrities provide readers with an opportunity to experience similarity identification and to use gossip narratives as a lens through which to consider and discuss their own experiences.

Indeed, many of the Cube readers report identifying with celebrities in this way. Lisa, a 30-year-old educator, Sasha, an educator who declined to reveal her age, and Stacey, a 37-year-old program coordinator, recall instances in which they felt stories about celebrities had a personal connection to their own lives:

Lisa: I really enjoy celebrity wedding photographs. I am looking forward to getting married eventually so that is something that I'm looking into myself. I want to see who was there, look at dresses, look at flowers.

Sasha: They go behind the scenes with these people and they find out things about their world and put it in the magazines. So if you like this [star], you'll zoom in and you'll say, for example, myself I'm a big animal activist and lover, "Oh! She likes dogs! I [like] this girl because I read in the magazine that she likes dogs." I do connect that way.

Stacey: I think you are fascinated [by] or comment on things that obviously have somewhat of a selfish connection to your life in some way. I always find it interesting when they do comparison diets of the day. I'm constantly dieting and things like that. And I do find that if somebody's in the room who's getting married or something or having a baby or knows somebody who's having a baby, [stories about pregnant stars] spark conversation.

Lisa, Sasha, and Stacey all recognize aspects of their own lives in celebrity narratives. As they engage in similarity identification with these famous women, the readers use gossip stories as a way to consider and negotiate their own experiences.

It is this type of identification that leads readers to develop parasocial relationships with celebrities. According to Horton and Wohl (1956), media users develop parasocial relationships when they interact with and respond to mass-mediated representations of people, like celebrities, as though engaged in an actual social relationship with those figures. Celebrity gossip magazines invite readers to develop precisely these types of relationships with the stars, calling them by their first name and using direct address and personal pronouns. The Cube readers respond accordingly, describing their own relationships with celebrities in parasocial terms:

Nikki: *I* was upset when Jen and Brad broke up. I was like, "Nooo!"

Amber: Yeah, I was too. I was too. And for that reason I do not like Angelina Jolie. [Laughs]. Can't stand her. I cannot stand her. I mean hard core. I can't stand her.

Stephanie: Jen, I feel bad for Jennifer Aniston. They're constantly putting her on the cover, talking about her and babies and whether she wants babies. "Oh is she pregnant?" I'm like, "Leave her alone already!"

The Cube readers feel deeply and personally invested in the lives of celebrity women, with whom they relate and identify. Through these parasocial relationships, readers not only develop a sense of connection with famous women, but also a sense of solidarity with a larger female cohort. Stacey, for example, notes that celebrity stories "create a little bit of common ground," allow readers to "share in people's joys and sorrows," and connect "to the human spirit." Similarly, Sasha says that "as a woman," she feels an emotional connection to famous females, irrespective of her personal opinions about those stars. The Cube readers enjoy the idea that women across the country (regardless of where they live, how famous they are, or how much they earn) are reading and talking about the same topics, week after week sharing an "intimate common world" in which women are the central actors and in which female experience is highlighted (Hermes, 1995: 132).[5] In this way, famous women collectivize the concerns of female readers, reassuring them that their own experiences are not singular, but shared.

The knowable community provides readers with the opportunity to consider and evaluate their own experiences, but it also provides them with tools for articulating those experiences. As Stacey's comments suggest, celebrity stories prompt readers to think, and talk, about their own lives. Up to this point, I have traced the ways in which celebrity gossip magazines hail readers as participants in an ongoing conversation between members of a kind of virtual extended family; however, recent scholarship suggests that audiences use magazines as a way of participating in real-world conversations with those who are physically and emotionally closest to them (Feasey, 2008; Johansson, 2006). In her study of the British celebrity magazine *heat*, Rebecca Feasey's participants describe celebrity trivia as a type of "ice-breaker," a tool for creating dialogue amongst like-minded, sociable people (2008: 692). Celebrity stories have a tendency to get people talking, to get the stories rolling, to get the gossiping going.

The term *gossip*, derived from the Old English "godsibb," meaning a godparent, was originally used to describe an individual whose membership in a family was bestowed, not born into, and who thereby possessed intimate details about family life, despite his or her outsider status (Tebbutt, 1995). Over the years, the term has evolved, and has been used to denote friendship, companionship and, eventually, talk. Today gossip is most often defined, not as convivial chit chat, but as trivial, petty, or malicious conversation, most often pursued by women. Despite its sordid reputation, gossip is also an important part of women's oral culture, as Deborah Jones puts it, a way of talking "between women in their roles as women," which allows participants to share secrets, form bonds, and collectively express dissatisfaction (1980: 194). Still, in order to gossip, one must have something, or someone, to gossip about. By providing readers with a knowable community of celebrities, gossip magazines afford women the opportunity to engage in the type of talk that Jones describes.

The Cube readers consider celebrity gossip magazines to be fundamentally sociable texts which, unlike novels, newspapers, and fashion magazines, invite interaction and engagement. Stacey explains:

> I would think it would be rude, right now, if I picked up a book and started reading while you were in the room. But if I started reading a gossip magazine, it's viewed as a little bit more socially accepted because it's something you can have more of a dialogue over. It's not as individual an activity.

As Stacey points out, reading celebrity tabloids in public often ignites conversation, which transforms the act of reading from an individual pastime to a social, communal engagement. John Fiske calls this type of talk, "when the meanings made [by fans] are spoken and shared within a face-to-face or oral culture," *enunciative productivity*, and argues that it is in this process of articulation that the pleasure of fandom lies (1992: 37–8).

Indeed, much of the pleasure that the Cube readers find in celebrity gossip is located not in the magazines themselves, but in the discussions generated by the act of reading. The mere mention of a recent headline sparks instant debate amongst the Cube women:

Mary: Any time that I'm in the staff lounge and there's more than one person reading the magazines, it sparks conversation. Somebody will say, "God, look at that person" or "Ooh, this is a cute dress."

Sasha: I tend to talk about the magazines with the people around me. I engage in long, intense, and serious conversations about different things in the magazines. Absolutely. . . . My fellow females, they're right on it, all over it. First couple of words, they know what I'm talking about. They're right there indulging with me.

Amber: In social situations like at happy hour, maybe the conversation will drop for a second and then I'll say, "Oh my god, did you see what Lindsay Lohan did?"

The readers' comments illustrate the way in which gossip about the knowable community of celebrities serves as a common point of entry into discussions between women, allowing them to socially engage their peers in an enjoyable way.

These conversations often revolve around emotion – how the star feels, how readers feel about the stars, and how readers would feel if placed in the situation that the star is facing. The Cube women enjoy discussing their emotional reaction to these narratives and often express strong opinions about the celebrities that they "love," "hate," or love to hate. During a conversation in their office, Amber and Nikki became engrossed in a deep discussion about the relationship between film stars Rachel McAdams and Ryan Gosling:

Amber: If you see two celebrities and you don't like them together, you're going to say, "Oh no, he shouldn't marry *her*."

Nikki: That is true.

Amber: If you don't like the celebrity woman who he's with you are going to say, "Eh, I don't like them together." For whatever reason, you've already formulated your opinion about that person . . . And then you decide whether or not you like them together. I know I do that. Or if you get used to two people together and then they break up and start a new relationship, you still want them to go back to that person. I know *I* did. I was very upset with Ryan Gosling and Rachel McAdams because I wanted them to live out *The Notebook* together.

Nikki: How cute were they together!

Amber: I couldn't handle it when they broke up! [Laughs] And I did *not* want to see them with anybody else. I did *not* like whomever else they were dating. I just didn't like it.

As they engage in this type of emotion-driven gossip, Nikki and Amber develop an empathetic relationship, not only with celebrities, but with one another, continuously reaffirming their solidarity. Nikki's interjections, while brief, support Amber's statements and confirm that the two women share similar opinions about the stars. For Nikki and Amber, this exchange is about much more than celebrity gossip; it is about legitimating each other's experiences, strengthening their friendship, and caring for one another's emotional well-being.

In her research on soap operas, Mary Ellen Brown finds that the conversation generated by soaps enables audiences to participate in what she calls a "feminine cultural community of fans." Soap operas are not so very different from gossip magazines; they highlight the personal, the emotional, and the feminine while providing viewers with a knowable community, a recurring cast of characters that collectivizes and articulates the concerns of female life. Brown finds that, for viewers, the pleasure of soap operas lies not in the text itself, but in the conversation and kinship with other fans that the text affords. Brown writes:

> The process of being a soap fan, however, is not always just the process of watching. For long periods at a time, some fans miss watching the soap but "keep up" with it through conversations with other fans. . . . The pleasure is not just the pleasure of seeing women's interests and concerns represented on the screen: rather it lies in the active and selective use of these representations in women's everyday lives and shared social experiences. The representations are only pleasurable insofar as they can be activated in this way. (1989: 169–71)

For the Cube women, as for Brown's viewers, the pleasure of the celebrity gossip magazine is primarily derived from the conversation and kinship that result from the purposeful use of the text, not in the particular celebrity, story, or magazine.

While some of the Cube readers are hesitant to discuss their own personal lives or to gossip about friends or family members, those same readers view gossip about celebrities as a harmless conversational tool. "You're not going to hurt anybody in this magazine," explains Mary, a 33-year-old manager at the Cube, who thinks of conversation about celebrities as a "safe" form of gossip. "They're not going to hear you. They don't know what you're thinking. They don't really care as long as you're going to the movies they're putting out." "Celebrity gossip is," as Gamson argues, "a much freer realm, much more game-like than acquaintance gossip: there are no repercussions and there is no account-ability" (1994: 176). Gossip about knowable celebrities, therefore, provides readers with a unique conversational opportunity; it acts as both springboard and shield, allowing readers to share their opinions and experiences while avoiding the potentially undesirable outcomes that may be associated with gossip about friends and acquaintances.

Celebrity gossip is not primarily about the brightest stars and the juiciest tidbits, but about the validation of women's relationships, pleasures, and concerns. The ordinary celebrity is critical to audience pleasure, not because she implies that anyone can be a star, but because she teaches us that *the star can be anyone*. The specific celebrities do not matter – Britney and Khloe, Jessica and Jen all serve the same purpose; they are a *tabula rasa* on to which readers can project and interpret their own experiences and emotions. "What is important about the stars," as celebrity theorist Richard Dyer writes, "is their typicality or representativeness" (1998: 47). As publicly knowable representations of specific social types, "ordinary" celebrities provide readers with a lens through which to view themselves. Gossip magazines are not, at their core, about the celebrity, "them," but rather, as the title of the genre's flagship magazine suggests, about *us, our* relationships, *our* children, *our* struggles. These stories, *our* stories, deeply matter.

It is for this reason that readers, like the stars and the magazines themselves, are invested in the maintenance of the ordinary celebrity. Still, while they enjoy reading about, discussing, and identifying with the experiences of famous females, the Cube women do not always agree with what the magazines have to offer. Although they find some of the genre's narratives appealing and enticing, they find others ridiculous and insulting. This is the contradictory nature of the magazines, and, indeed, of the popular feminine. Yes, we enjoy the escape but still we feel guilty. Sure, we take pleasure in the gossip but we're a bit fed up with all those catfights. And of course we identify with these stars but why are they all slender, heterosexual, and obsessed with babies?

Celebrity gossip magazines, like *Oprah* and *General Hospital* and this week's *Lifetime* movie, address women's contradictory experiences of female life and femininity and provide a safe space in which discussions of these experiences are encouraged. But popular feminine texts often re-present women's experiences in ways that are stereotypic, narrow-minded, and retrograde. Celebrity gossip magazines are no exception. How, then, do readers reconcile the pleasures that they find in the genre with their often adverse reaction to the narrow scripts that it offers? The next chapters explore how readers respond to the magazines' normative codes, discussing and dissecting them in ways that render the act of reading pleasurable.

4
Making Morality Meaningful

"Shame on Lindsay!" blasts the cover of *Life & Style*'s September 28, 2009, issue, which scolds 23-year-old starlet Lindsay Lohan for allegedly introducing her teenage sister Ali to "drugs," "diet pills," and "plastic surgery," for "ruin[ing] her own life and now . . . endangering baby sister Ali's." The headline is paired with a photo of "Angelina" [Jolie] looking "scary skinny" and a fashion story touting "fall's lipo jeans," designed to make you "look 10 lbs slimmer!" This montage is indicative of the celebrity gossip genre's penchant for emphatically prescribing contradictory messages about how female celebrities (and readers) should behave. Week after week, the magazines present guidelines, specific rules and instructions, aimed at ordinary women and the stars who are "just like us." Be thin, but not too thin. Be fashionable, but be yourself. Have fun, but don't get into trouble. Enjoy sex, but don't be too promiscuous. As Douglas argues, "Celebrity journalism drives home the message that the gender tightrope for women is gossamer-thin and precarious. And celebrity journalism claims to tell women – the visible famous ones and the invisible rest of us – how to walk it" (2010: 246).

This chapter examines the normative, moral codes that celebrity gossip magazines re-present and perpetuate, and the ways in which readers make sense of this endless stream of competing ideals. How is it that women find such stories appealing? What is it about these narratives that allows readers to ignore, or at least put aside, these troublesome messages long enough to enjoy the act of reading? What makes us go back and purchase next week's issue?

Ordinary Ideals: Celebrity Gossip as Moral Tale

Despite the motif of the "normal," ordinary celebrity, gossip magazines emphasize and glorify extreme versions of femininity. The stories they tell are about what American culture considers to be the most beautiful, talented, and financially successful women in the world. However, like many other forms of popular media, the magazines do not present these women as the exception, but as the rule. Celebrities are depicted as normal, and therefore the ideals they embody are made to appear achievable. But gossip narratives are not only stories of aspiration (of hope, achievement, and potential); they are also stories of foreboding (of failure, ambition gone awry, and squandered opportunity).

Celebrity stories can be understood as fables, not unlike those told by Aesop or the Brothers Grimm (Bird, 1976; Brewer, 2009; Chancey, 1999; Dégh, 1994). "Not only are [tabloid narratives] revealing tales," writes Ian Connell, in his analysis of celebrities in the popular media, "but also tales which set out to teach moral lessons by exposing unworthy and unbecoming actions" (1992: 77). Applied to female celebrities in the pages of the gossip press, such stories, as folklorist Linda Dégh writes, reproduce fable-like notions of gender roles, wherein women are taught to be passive, demure, and obedient to men so as to achieve an idealized form of femininity, grounded in fulfilling one's role as a wife and mother. These narratives provide readers with a kind of cultural compass, which instructs them on how to navigate the tricky waters of "appropriate" femininity; however, these "ideals" are not unique to the celebrity gossip genre, but a reflection and exaggeration of broader cultural and mediated messages about female life.

Such moral tales have been a staple of celebrity magazines for decades. Fan magazines of the early twentieth century featured stories about the homes, marriages, children, and families of the stars, in an effort to make actors appear ordinary and wholesome. Yet, by the 1920s, celebrities' domestic problems were generating scandalous headlines (deCordova, 1990). Marital disputes, divorces, rendezvous, and sexual liaisons have been hot gossip ever since (McLean, 1995). As deCordova writes:

> It should not be surprising that a system of discourse driven by a logic of secrecy (and revelation) would light upon the sexual as the ultimate secret – particularly since the truth of the star's identity had already been located in the realm of the private. The star system, and arguably twentieth-century culture in general, depends on an interpretative schema that equates identity with the private and furthermore accords the sexual the status of the most private, and thus the most truthful, locus of identity. (1990: 140)

Indeed, sexual relations between celebrities remain a primary topic of discussion in gossip magazines (stories about romantic relationships appear, you recall, most frequently on recent covers).

We see moral tales about sexual behavior activated in recent stories of celebrity romance. Take, for instance, a November 5, 2012, story in *Us Weekly*, which provides readers with a first-hand account of Justin Timberlake's wedding to Jessica Biel. The article, which features images of the smiling couple and the "magical" Italian chapel and ceremony grounds where they wed, reads as follows:

> At the heart of the Borgo Egnazia resort on the Adriatic coast of Puglia, Italy, is a chapel straight out of a fairy tale, complete with bell tower. On October 19, 150 guests gathered to watch Jessica Biel, in a white Giambattista Valli gown with pink accents, glide down a spiral staircase and pledge her devotion to Justin Timberlake. After the beaming couple exchanged traditional vows and were declared "man and wife" as the clock struck 7:30 P.M., the crowd let out a collective cheer to cue an avalanche of heart-shaped petals. The ceremony capped off a story-book week for friends and family . . . Sparing no expense, the couple flew bleary-eyed guests back to the U.S. via private jet the next day. "I'd say it all cost about $2 million!" marvels the guest. The pair are already planning their next epic production: parenthood.

Here, romance is a fairy story, complete with clocks chiming, spiral staircases, and waves of magical petals falling down upon the happy couple. The syntax of the narrative even suggests a script, referring to the event as a "production." Further, Timberlake and Biel's wedding, or at least the depiction of it that *Us* presents, is based on images of "traditional," heteronormative romance, wherein the female "pledges" herself to her husband, and on an ethos of conspicuous consumption. The outcome of all this is not only love and marriage, but also the presumed birth of a child. Now that Jessica has taken up her role as wife, motherhood is made to seem inevitable.

Yet gossip stories also show the flip side of the fairy tale. Woe is the star who cheats on her boyfriend or the "home-wrecking" woman who leads a man to infidelity. One need look no further than the star of the popular vampire-themed series *Twilight*, actress Kristen Stewart. Stewart was ridiculed as a "Trampire" in 2012 when news broke that she had had a sexual affair with the director of one of her films, in spite of her relationship with long-time boyfriend, co-star Robert Pattinson. A July 2012 cover of *Us Weekly* shouts in capitalized, canary-yellow letters, "KRISTEN CHEATS ON ROB!" and claims that the young actress's "steamy affair" was caught on camera. The "slut-shaming" that subsequently ensued sends a clear lesson: women who do not fit into "appropriate" moral scripts are subject to scrutiny and ridicule (Lang, 2012).[1]

These codes are also applied to famous females who act in less obviously subversive ways. In a January 4, 2010, issue of *In Touch*, the magazine dissects pop star Britney Spears's relationship with boyfriend Jason Trawick. The story, entitled, "Britney is Pressuring Jason To Get Married," claims that Spears wants her boyfriend to work less so that they can spend more time together and eventually wed (Brit can financially support their family herself, thank you very much). But, it seems, Britney cannot be both the successful breadwinner and the happy wife. "If Britney keeps it up," we learn, "she may wind up not getting married at all" because "Jason's career is very important to him . . . and he doesn't want to make a choice between Britney and his career. Plus, Jason clearly doesn't like being pressured to commit." Here, Britney is presented as a pushy, overzealous girlfriend and an emotional wreck – we are also told, in a photo montage, that she finds her children overwhelming, "craves constant contact," engages in unhealthy eating habits, and gets "emotional" in public places. To top it all off, she's pictured wearing five wedding rings! Clearly Prince Charming will not fall for her. Thus, readers learn that a "happy ending" is possible, but only for those who adhere to particular codes of appearance and behavior. Women who are beautiful, faithful, and selfless, who yearn for nothing more than a breadwinning husband and a gaggle of babies, are destined for happiness. Those who don't follow this script are doomed to experience failure and rejection.

But while narratives about romance and sex continue to dominate the genre, contemporary magazines have taken up a new site of scandal. If twentieth-century gossip was defined by its obsession with sexuality (and the sexual self as the most private, most guarded, and most truthful element of self), twenty-first-century gossip adds an obsession with the female body. Star narratives have long relied on the representation of the celebrity body, and audience interpretations of celebrity are deeply tied to the physical self (Dyer, 2003); however, today's celebrity gossip magazines zealously track minute changes in the form, color, shape, and display of female bodies and body parts in a manner that has not been heretofore seen. The genre's surveillance of the female body takes many forms (think of those "Beach Body" headlines and plastic surgery before-and-afters), but is more clearly articulated in the pregnancy narrative. It is in the notorious "baby bump watch" that the sexual self, and the potential for scandal that sexuality portends, intersects with the bodily self, with all of its possibilities for revolt. It is here, therefore, that celebrity women are subject to the most neurotic level of scrutiny.

Meredith Nash traces the representation of Britney Spears's pregnancy, and the backlash that occurred as Britney's body transformed from "taut and tight to 'fat' and even 'grotesque'," and notes that Spears's pregnancy served as a kind of "collective cultural experience" through which ideas about femininity and women's social roles were, quite literally, embodied (2005/2006: 27). Since actress Demi Moore appeared pregnant, naked, and draped in jewels on the cover of *Vanity Fair* in 1991, the bodies of pregnant celebrities have become increasingly available for display and public viewing (Britney struck a similar nude pose on the cover of *Harper's Bazaar* in August 2006; an array of starlets have followed suit). Not only do these representations serve as "visually verifiable" evidence of the stars' private lives, but they also contribute to a discourse that works to police the female body (Knee, 2006). The bump watch, it seems, is all around us, ready to aim a hot pink arrow at the midsection of any woman who crosses its path. This "watch" is, quite simply, a form of surveillance that, as Meyers writes, "is rooted in the idea that *only* a pregnant woman could justifiably have a bump and *only* a woman in a heterosexual relationship could justifiably be pregnant." Further, "as a gossip game, the bump watch positions the female celebrity body as the embodiment of idealized feminine sexuality and physicality and uses the potential of a bump as a means to police that body through gossip talk that recuperates wayward female subjects through ridicule and shame" (2012: 59).

Celebrity gossip magazines produce a powerful discourse around pregnancy, motherhood, and the pregnant body, which may be especially salient for the genre's readership, many of whom may be pregnant or thinking about the possibility of pregnancy (the average age for a woman to become pregnant with her first child in 2010 was between 25 and 26 years old, an age which correlates with that of the genre's target readership).[2] Stories about pregnant celebrities aim a sharply discerning eye at expecting mothers and, because "pregnancy, as socially portrayed, epitomizes femininity," these narratives not only shape our popular understanding and expectations for expectant mothers, but for all women (Graham, 1976).

The tone of the pregnancy narrative depends on the degree to which the expectant celeb adheres to or fails to meet the moral standards set out by the magazine. While some behaviors, such as avoiding alcohol and tobacco and eating nutritious foods, are essential to the health of mother and child, other personal choices are not innately positive or negative, although the magazines consistently present them as such. Women who adhere to the moral codes of the magazine are

Table 4.1 Heroic vs failed mothers

Heroic mothers	Failed mothers
Married/monogamous	Single/promiscuous
Ideal weight	Overweight/underweight
Happy	Troubled
Wealthy	Poor[3]
"Mild"	"Wild"
Selfless	Selfish

depicted as heroic mothers; those who fail to meet these strict standards are criticized and portrayed as failures.

Pregnancy narratives often focus on the mother's appearance, weight, romantic relationships, and lifestyle choices. Stories featuring heroic moms emphasize the woman's beauty and "healthy" weight, her positive habits, her monogamous (almost always heterosexual) relationship, her happiness, her financial ability to care for her children (the fact that celebrity women are extremely wealthy goes without saying), and her desire to be a good mother. Alternatively, stories about failed mothers focus on the woman's weight gain or loss, poor choices, unhappy romances or infidelity, recklessness, and selfishness. Heroic mothers take care of themselves and others; failed mothers "let themselves go." Heroic mothers are celebrated, praised, and doted upon; failed mothers are criticized, mocked, and condemned. Pregnancy narratives serve as a powerful moral tale. They teach readers about which bodies, behaviors, and emotional responses garner respect and admiration, and which deserve punishment. Juxtaposed with those celebrities who manage to negotiate the tricky terrain of "appropriate" female behavior, failed mothers serve as a warning to all women: follow the rules or you too will be scorned.

This moral framework is further emphasized by a third type of pregnancy narrative, a Cinderella story of sorts, which tells of a woman who is, through her pregnancy, transformed from a selfish, unattractive party girl to a selfless, beautiful, sophisticated woman. Celebrities such as Nicole Richie, Angelina Jolie, Lily Allen, and *Jersey Shore* star

Snooki have all been presented as transgressors who, through pregnancy, have "turned their lives around" and "found happiness." A September 2009 issue of *Us Weekly* clearly outlines this transformative process, featuring interviews with pregnant reality stars Kendra Baskett and Kourtney Kardashian, both of whom have allegedly undergone a mommy-makeover. The introduction to the article reads:

> What a difference a pregnancy makes. Ten months ago, Kendra Baskett, 24, was a Playboy model cavorting nude inside Hugh Hefner's legendary mansion. Flash to today: She's preparing for the arrival of her first child (Henry Baskett IV) with NFL player husband Hank Baskett, 27, whom she wed June 27. Kourtney Kardashian did a similar 180. Her life as a single Miami party girl came to a screeching halt when she learned she was expecting with her on-again beau, entrepreneur Scott Disick, 26.

Accompanying photographs show the two women embracing their partners, referred to as "Doting Dads-to-be" and trading Porsches for minivans, alcohol for bedtime snacks, and *Playboy* mansions for, well, regular mansions. Once "wild," now "mild," Kendra and Kourtney have allegedly given up the bad habits of yesteryear and embraced their role as mothers; in doing so, they have earned both personal satisfaction and public respect. This transformation narrative reinforces binaries around appropriate and transgressive femininities while suggesting that all women, regardless of their past misdeeds, can become heroic mothers (i.e., good women) if only they, too, engage in socially sanctioned behaviors.

Post-pregnancy weight-loss stories, also a popular feature, perform a similar function, reincorporating the transgressive female and her body through an ethos of self-regimentation. For instance, a January 2013 issue of *Us Weekly* features a cover story about Kourtney Kardashian, now a mother of two, who went "from baby to bikini in 6 months!" The caption below a photo of pregnant Kourtney claims the star gained 45 pounds while expecting her daughter; meanwhile, a two-page spread shows a slender, bikini-clad Kourtney lying on a sofa. The story tells how the reality star practiced yoga and dance cardio, jogged, did crunches, juiced, drank green tea, refrained from alcohol, and ate clarified butter to

Figure 4.1 Transformed Transgressors, *Us Weekly*,
September 7, 2009, pp. 48–53. Courtesy of Wenner Media.
All rights reserved. Reprinted by permission

regain her figure. This story and others like it also emphasize
the love between heterosexual parents and the relationship
between mother and child, all the while making it clear that
famous women are subject to rigorous regimentation, not
only during their pregnancies, but also in their everyday roles
as wives and mothers. In making these standards clear and
available to the reader, celebrity gossip magazines reinforce
the idea that ordinary women – remember, celebrities are, in
this context, "ordinary" – must be constantly wary of their
own bodies and behaviors lest they be caught making the
"wrong" choices. The message here is clear: you, dear reader,
are, like Kendra and Kourtney, being judged at all times.

However, many of the codes set out by the magazines are
dynamic. Some moms-to-be who gain weight are said to be

sacrificing their body image for the health of their child; others are criticized for not taking better care of themselves. Some single moms are celebrated for their perseverance and love of children while others are portrayed as irresponsible. Once again, the moral tightrope is thin and slippery. As Douglas writes:

> Nowhere is the gap between image and reality wider than the one separating the smiling, serene, financially comfortable, and perfectly coiffed media mom from her frazzled, exhausted, sputum-covered, real-life counterpart. Like all other messages surrounding us – about sex, about assertiveness, about women in politics, and about independence – the messages about motherhood and babies crash into each other like tidal waves . . . Once again we find ourselves under surveillance, not only as sex objects, or as workers, but as mothers. And on all sides of us are voices with megaphones, yelling completely opposite things to us. (1994: 280, 283)

Making Morality Meaningful

Gossip stories present a rigid set of moral codes, which tell readers how to act, what to look like, and even how to feel. Yet the moral codes displayed here are not unique to the genre; these tales cull together and make explicit many of the feminine ideals that permeate contemporary American culture writ large. The Cube women are deeply aware of these codes, at times comparing themselves to the "norms" presented in the magazines. Mary, for instance, reports looking to celebrities for what she calls a "barometer of normality":

> I think women are looking in these magazines for barometers of what's normal or what they should expect in their own lives . . . Who doesn't like [it] when you drive past a house with the windows and blinds open and the lights on? Who's not going to look in? This is your way of looking in [on] people . . . People want to know that what they're doing is OK, isn't far out of the realm of traditional, mainstream normalcy. These magazines, with the privacy broken down, give that, possibly fake, look into other people's lives for you to see whether or not you measure up. . . . You want to see if you're normal like they're normal.

Mary finds a sense of comfort in comparing herself to female celebrities. And indeed, the magazines' stories offer a reassuring roadmap. At times, readers find celebrity gossip to be a pleasurable escape, a window into a world where good and bad are clearly defined, men are either gushing and doting or obviously evil, and monetary concerns do not exist. Many of the Cube women describe this type of reading as a mode of stress relief. Helena likens her own reading experience to that of watching a movie saying, "It's an escape for a couple of hours. You get to escape your life and go into somebody else's life. Reading is another way of escaping."

But readers' comfortable escape to celebrity-land is often coupled with feelings of self-doubt and anxiety about their own inability to meet the magazines' set criteria. Readers are not immune to these powerful messages; even the most self-confident amongst the Cube women do, at times, feel pressure to "measure up" to the standards set by celebrities, despite an awareness that these hyper-idealized images are problematic, that the moralities set out by the magazines are deeply flawed, and that the "norms" they promote are not, in actuality, representative of ordinary women.

The Cube readers therefore struggle with a desire to embrace and enjoy the magazines on the one hand, and a rejection of the genre's normative messages on the other. Amber, Sasha, and Helena all take pleasure in reading celebrity gossip magazines, but nevertheless express skepticism and frustration toward the genre's surveillance of women, lack of racial and ethnic diversity, and prescriptive attitude toward female behavior:

Amber: I think they should just leave people alone in certain situations. But it's a catch-22 because I like to read about it, but I think it's wrong. I *hate* that they're stalking Sandra Bullock. I hate that. But I read every little article I see about how they're stalking Sandra Bullock! [Laughs]

Sasha: There *is* diversity in celebrity gossip magazines but I would like to see more. When I open the magazine, I always scan to see if there's a woman of color in the line-up because usually there is *not*. They could have ten slots and not one of them will be a woman of color or maybe *only* one will be

. . . I will read her article first because I find that I need to connect with something that's about *me*. I feel like, if they really want people like myself to read more of them, they need to give more of that. To be fair, I *am* seeing more diversity. I turn to a page and there's pretty Halle Berry. You have this girl Zoe [Saldana] who's coming up and Jennifer Hudson is all over the place and she's quite chocolate. So yeah, I do feel that it's diverse but it could be more.

Helena: if a woman has a child outside of marriage that gets blown up. If a woman gets married on a fling, like Britney Spears did, that gets blown up. I think that it should be all what a woman wants to do. Jennifer Aniston, for example, she's perfectly [capable] of having a baby. If it just doesn't happen for her [that's OK] . . . That's what I felt like I would do if I got to be 30, 31, 32, 33. If I was 40 and single I'd want to have a child too. It's interesting because I would want to adopt because I feel like there's a lot of other children who need mothers who were cast aside.

While Amber, Sasha, and Helena discuss a variety of topics, they all express a similar response to the act of reading celebrity gossip magazines. All three vocalize their desire to enjoy celebrity gossip, but note that this desire is moderated by a recognition that the genre's treatment of women – its relentless pursuit of the most personal details of our lives, the narrow version of ideal femininity that it paints, and the strict, heteronormative timeline that it so ardently holds us to – is deeply flawed. It seems bizarre, then, to think that women would want to spend their free time reading these magazines. How can celebrity stories, which obsess, nitpick, and scrutinize us be fun (even relaxing) to read? How could it possibly be pleasurable to engage in these kinds of tales?

"It Makes My Life Seem a Lot Better"

One of the ways in which the Cube women transform their discomfort with the genre's feminine codes into moments of pleasurable engagement is through feelings of *schadenfreude*.

The German word *schadenfreude* refers to the pleasure we feel in the misfortunes of other people and, although *schadenfreude* may seem to connote malice, Portmann argues that it is actually a sentiment that draws on a variety of human emotions and is deeply tied to our ideas about social standards of moral appropriateness. Tracing the ways in which, like gossip, *schadenfreude* has been linked with women, Portmann draws from Alison Jaggar's theory of outlaw emotions to situate the *schadenfreude* of women within a broader social context. Outlaw emotions are those emotional responses that are incompatible with "dominant perceptions and values in a community" (Portmann, 2000: 176). "People do not always experience conventionally acceptable emotions," writes Portmann. "They may feel satisfaction rather than embarrassment when their leaders make foolish mistakes; they may feel revulsion toward socially sanctioned ways of privileging men . . . the *schadenfreude* of women is largely justified [under patriarchy]" (192, 196). It is, perhaps, unsurprising then that the Cube readers take pleasure in the misfortunes of female celebrities, who are held up as unattainable models of those cultural ideals that are, often, unsatisfying and oppressive to women.

In her study of gossip magazine reading, Hermes also finds that women use stories about the misfortunes of celebrities as a way of commiserating and of comforting their own sense of self (1995: 300). More recent work on the British tabloid *heat* suggests that readers feel a sense of "frustration, resentment, and anger" toward idealized images of celebrities and that "celebrity bashing" allows audiences to distance themselves from the alleged "normality" of the stars, cope with their own anxieties, and revel in a "momentary experience of power and control" (Johansson, 2006). Similarly, the Cube readers, aware of the impossibly high standards to which women are held and frustrated by their own inability to live up to those standards, revel in instances in which the stars are presented in an unflattering light, as fallible individuals rather than as glossy idols. "We almost want to see them look bad because they always look so good," explains Cynthia. "We want to say, 'Oh, she got a nose job' or 'Oh my god, she looks terrible in that' or 'Oh, she got fat' because we would all really like to be in their position in life. So we tend to criticize because we're jealous. There you go." Mary, Nikki, and Stephanie shared similar reactions:

Mary: In some ways, it makes me feel good that people who are supposedly successful and who are held up by society as being models are struggling with the same issues that I am . . . I know that the magazines are catering to that piece of everybody that wants to hear the problems. Because we've got problems too.

Nikki: We talk about who's going to jail. Who's having a nervous breakdown. I enjoy hearing about those. Failures. It makes my life seem a lot better. It also seems that I'm not as crazy.

Stephanie: [It's a] way of feeling a little bit better about ourselves because we're like, "Look at her! Did you see her in that magazine? She's not that hot. She acts like she's all that but she needs to work on her stomach!" [Laughs]. If *she's* wearing a bikini I should not even think twice! *I* should wear a bikini! Why did I put mine away!

Confronted with an endless parade of exceptionally thin, gorgeous, and wealthy celebs, readers express their frustration with these unrealistic "norms" by taking pleasure in celebrity failure. The idea that even rich and famous women find it difficult to live up to strict feminine ideals provides readers with a welcome, if temporary, relief from the strain of these moral codes. In addition, when celebrities make major life mistakes – committing crimes, losing millions, or maxing out on plastic surgery – it makes readers' own alleged inadequacies seem minor by comparison.

The magazines are, in fact, designed to encourage this type of reading; they position audiences as adjudicators in their moral universe, offer up generous helpings of less-than-flattering tidbits and images, and invite readers to weigh in (remember those "Who wore it best?" polls?). One of the stories that readers often cite as the meanest and most critical – the "Worst Beach Body" photo spread – is also a staple of the genre. The purpose of this type of story, which typically appears in summertime issues and is comprised of large, full-color paparazzi photos of mostly female stars looking "Hot" or "Not" in swimwear, is to allow readers to compare their own bodies with those of famous women and to critique the stars' flaws. "Although people might tell you, 'Oh that's mean! We won't read that,' those issues with [unflattering] bikini covers actually do really well," according to photo editor Susanne Rieth. Indeed, the Cube women enjoy these types of stories, which illustrate the negative elements of fame, and use tales of celebrity failure as a way of temporarily blocking out their troubles. Cube readers like Nikki report that stories about celebrity weight problems, jail time, and nervous breakdowns, "make life seem a lot better."

But while *schadenfreude* allows readers to temporarily bolster their own self-esteem, this pleasure does nothing to challenge the standards that the Cube women are resisting. Rather, these narratives and the gossip that they engender pit women, the famous and the ordinary, against one another in a constant scramble. The outcome of this gossip is highly polarizing: it leaves some women (the richest, prettiest, most desirable, and therefore closest to fitting the so-called norm) at the top, and the others (those who fail to meet those criteria) at the bottom. In reality, this balancing act does not benefit anyone, but rather reproduces a constant form of surveillance and judgment, of both one's self and others, that assures no woman can ever truly measure up.

Figure 4.2 "Best & Worst Beach Bodies," *Star*, March 26, 2012. Courtesy of American Media, Inc. All rights reserved. Reprinted by permission

Still, readers don't always engage in "celebrity bashing" when rejecting the genre's codes of femininity. Many of the Cube readers view the magazines' normative frames not as influential models to be applied to one's self, but as wrong-headed, overtly ridiculous opinions, deserving of critique. In a conversation about reality star Heidi Montag (who, at the age of 23, reportedly had 10 plastic surgeries performed in one day), Nikki and Stacey discuss the pleasure that they find in the "ridiculousness" of celebrity stories:

Nikki: It's fun to critique because you realize how crazy [celebrities] are . . . Like Heidi [Montag]. How she thinks she looks good and she's only 23 and yet she's had 10 to 15 plastic surgeries. I'm just laughing at you because you *don't* look good.

Stacey: Everybody's had a comment like, "That's ridiculous." Like Heidi and her big boobs. Or Angelina, "Really, like, you're going to adopt *another* baby?" So some of [the fun] is you seeing the ridiculousness of it.

For Nikki and Stacey, the pleasure of reading lies not only in "seeing" the absurdity of the so-called norms that circulate around famous women, but also in the ability to call these versions of femininity out for what readers feel they truly are – ridiculous. In this way, the Cube women are able to identify the codes of femininity with which they disagree and to scoff and ridicule these codes as they engage with the magazines. The Cube women do express these types of critiques when reading alone, but they are most likely to challenge the magazines' claims when reading, and gossiping, with other women in a group setting. In these moments of collective engagement, dissatisfaction develops into a subject of shared contemplation and discussion.

Gossip has been shown to function as a form of social control, a way of establishing and policing social norms (Gluckman, 1963; Levin and Arluke, 1987; Rysman, 1977). Our first inclination, therefore, might be to suspect that the gossip generated by celebrity magazines would result in readers maintaining the social norms that the genre dictates. Because these "norms" are so explicitly stated and so firmly reinforced, week after week, it would be natural to assume that magazine-generated gossip reinforces these frameworks.

When the Cube women gossip about celebrities, their conversations often do address the social norms outlined by the magazines and, indeed, readers do engage in a kind of consensus-building around these norms. However, the consensus-building they partake in does not simply mirror the ideological messages put forth by the magazines. Often, readers openly reject the genre's moral world, expressing frustration with its overwhelmingly white, wealthy, heterosexual, and thin version of femininity and empathizing with female celebrities who are subject to the obsessive glare of the tabloid spotlight. As readers gossip about celebrities, they vocalize their dissatisfaction. In the staff lounge, Stacey and Helena engage in this form of contestation gossip as they discuss the genre's emphasis on celebrities' weight:

Stacey: I *hate* when they take pictures of these poor girls' cellulite! [hitting the table] . . . They could be sitting the wrong way and it's like, they create major, major body issues for the celebrities and for women. And I just don't like that . . . Even though you're drawn to looking at whose butt is that with the cellulite! [Laughs] You just feel like, "*Really?* Did they deserve that?" They probably were just sitting and the sun was glaring on their leg. Everybody has some. It makes us crazy, women crazy.

Helena: They have these terrible pictures. Pictures like this [with celebrity cellulite] make me want to turn it over. It's degrading to somebody because it doesn't matter who you are, if you have these kinds of fat you are still going to be degraded and you're still going to be pushed down and all this negativity placed upon you. There are all these stereotypes of how women should look. That's not right. Then there's all these skinny-ass models who are teeny tiny and they still have to lose five pounds! Are you kidding – they're going to fall over and die! Well, Jessica Simpson's overweight? What, are you kidding me, she's gorgeous! What are you talking about she's overweight? She's got gorgeous curves and so what if she's 5 or 10 pounds over what the perfect, quote unquote perfect, is. If she's happy with herself, she's happy with herself. What is the problem with it? . . . I don't like when they have bad pictures of celebrities without their make-up. "She looks so horrible without her make-up!" Well, so she's human! They're all human people. I don't know how people expect others to be completely perfect.

Through their discussion, Stacey and Helena not only express their disagreement with the magazines' depiction of women's bodies, but also reaffirm a shared understanding that women should not be subject to such harsh critiques of their physical appearance. In this way, Stacey and Helena do use gossip to establish and maintain normative codes; however, the codes that they subscribe to are self-generated ones, which reflect their own common values. Further, as readers engage in consensus-building around these codes, they are able to establish and maintain social relationships and reaffirm and strengthen friendships (Coates, 1989).

At times, debates about specific values and norms develop into discussions of broader topics and personal opinions. In these instances, readers use celebrity stories as a way of generating conversations and expressing their own perspectives on many of the social issues featured in the magazines, including divorce, stalking, and drug abuse. Danielle recalls an instance in which a story about celebrity infidelity sparked a debate amongst coworkers:

> Sometimes conversation about the magazines leads into conversation about real life. Oh yes, it does. Even the other day we were all in there talking about Sandra Bullock, Tiger Woods, and all that stuff, and Taj blurts out, "Well, you mean to tell me you never flirted with somebody, or something that would make your significant other jealous?" And then it gets into these personal things about how people really feel and what they've really done . . . I don't think these conversations would come up without the magazines [since there was a] diverse group of people that happened to be there at the time. I really don't think we would gather together to gossip about stuff if there wasn't something to spur that on.

Here, celebrity gossip stories act as a point of entry into broader conversations about personal responsibility, character, and values, allowing readers to consider, clarify, and contribute their opinions.

At the time that I met with the Cube women, one story that readers found especially salient was the ongoing coverage of the relationship between pop singer Rihanna and her on-again, off-again boyfriend, rapper Chris Brown, who had been accused of physically assaulting Rihanna in early 2009. This story ignited intense debate about domestic violence amongst the Cube women. Stacey describes an experience that she shared with her sister after the allegations against Brown became public:

> My sister and I just went out to a club recently and she requested the song "Forever" and the DJ said, "I can't play that anymore because people hate Chris Brown." And my sister was like, "That's so true." We started getting in a conversation about [the] domestic violence with Chris Brown and what happens to his career now. It's interesting how during that time the magazines spun that. [Rihanna's story] probably was a vehicle for young girls to realize maybe that they weren't in [healthy relationships]. I think [celebrity magazines] create dialogue about important issues by taking it away from something about you and placing it on other people, which makes it a little bit more comfortable or lighthearted having the conversation. But the root of [the topic] is still being discussed in some sort of way. I normally wouldn't bring up domestic abuse in the staff lounge but if I'm reading a story about Rihanna like, "Oh my god, isn't it horrible what happened to her!" and someone will say, "Oh, I know somebody who that happened to" and I think, "Oh, get out!" So there is this dialogue that is sparked, important dialogue that women need to talk about.

Stacey's narrative shows how stories about the personal lives of celebrities can prompt significant discussions about social issues. "Young girls are watching what Rihanna does more than they are watching the news to see what's happening to everyday people," says Amber, who feels that Rihanna's story helped "shed light" on the issue of domestic violence.

Celebrity stories invite the Cube women to assess the behaviors of famous women and, through those assessments, to define and articulate their own personal opinions. Many of the readers were upset, for example, to later learn that

Rihanna and Chris Brown had reportedly reconciled, not only because they were concerned for Rihanna's well-being, but also because they felt that her actions would send a troubling message, a message with which they disagreed, about how women should respond to physically and mentally abusive partners. Expressed together with friends and peers who share their concerns, the Cube women's individual perspectives were reinforced and made all the more salient.

And while domestic abuse is not typically the focus of celebrity journalism, stories about marriage, friendship, mental health, aging, sex, and body image are mainstays of the genre. These topics are typically excluded from mainstream news, and even from "proper" conversation, because they are "private" matters. Yet they are also serious subjects, subjects that women *want* to talk about. These topics deeply matter to the Cube readers, who welcome the opportunity to engage with these issues. "I think women are obviously interested in things that have far more substance than gossip," says Mary, "but these topics in real life have substance. How you feel about your own body or your relationship and if you're secure or whether or not your boyfriend or girlfriend is going to cheat on you? Those are pretty weighty topics." Despite the serious nature of these subjects, the conversations that ensue are not depressing or hostile, but engaging and sociable. The Cube women appreciate and enjoy the opportunity to discuss serious issues in a lighthearted manner; indeed, it is this opportunity for discussion that draws many of the Cube women to the magazines week after week.

The pleasure of celebrity gossip lies not in the passive acceptance of the genre's fable-like mores, but in the opportunity for conversation and self-expression that the magazines provide. Readers enjoy talking back to the fairy tale, urging the protagonist not to give up her voice for that no-good prince, not to believe that being the fairest of them all is the only route to a happy ending. By comparing and contrasting their behaviors with those of famous females and vocalizing their opinions and concerns, readers are able to make a claim for their own values and write their own moral codes, both individually, and in concert with other women. But why do readers feel that they have the authority to challenge the text in the first place? What is it about celebrity gossip magazines that makes them so easily contestable and gives readers the power to talk back? How do these texts, despite their prescriptive codes, manage to function as a forum for dissent? The answer lies in the ambiguous truthfulness of the celebrity gossip genre.

5
Ambiguously Truthful

In January 2001, just 10 months after *Us Weekly*'s debut, George W. Bush was sworn in as the 43rd president of the United States. His electoral defeat of the incumbent vice-president, Al Gore (who won the popular vote), hinged on a highly contested recount of ballots in Florida, where Bush's younger brother, Jeb, happened to be Governor.[1] Many wondered whether the results of the election were accurate, or whether the true victor could even be determined. Nine months later, nearly 3,000 people were killed when al-Qaeda suicide bombers drove two airliners into the twin towers of New York City's World Trade Center in one of the most devastating attacks ever committed on US soil. During the seven years that followed, America engaged in three wars: one rhetorical war on terror and two very real wars in Iraq and Afghanistan.

It is within this socio-political milieu that celebrity gossip magazines came to dominate American news-stands. Although *Us Weekly*'s 2000 debut originally disappointed – with profits failing to meet initial expectations – in the months following 9/11, sales soared. By 2002, *Us* had achieved the 10th largest circulation growth amongst mass-market magazines, drawing over a million readers each week.[2] That same year, the celebrity weekly marketplace began to expand as Bauer Publishing launched *In Touch Weekly*, which featured content and aesthetics nearly identical to that of *Us*. By the time Bush was re-elected in 2004, Bonnie Fuller had helped to usher *Star* into the genre's growing ranks and Bauer added *Life & Style* to its roster.

Why did celebrity gossip appeal to so many after 9/11? Douglas argues that, in the wake of the terrorist attacks, our engagement with celebrity news was akin to pulling "a big collective quilt over our heads." Celebrity gossip "was a lot less scary and confusing than stories about al-Qaeda. We could talk about it with anyone without getting into a political fight, and we could use it to affirm our own opinions about right and wrong" (2010: 250). Even for the politically engaged, celebrity news offered a break from the incessant coverage of war. As Bonnie Fuller told LXTV in 2007, readers who care "very much" about world affairs "can still relax and kick back with *Star* magazine and care about baby Suri's pictures"[3] "Remember when Sept. 11 was going to kill frivolity?" pondered Jon Fine in 2004, as he named *Us Weekly* magazine of the year. "Neither do we."[4]

Celebrity journalism also offered audiences a relief from the president's hypermasculine personae. Bush cast himself as a cowboy-hat-wearing American everyman, performing a rough-and-tumble, guy's guy form of heteronormative masculinity that defined his presidency (Gutterman and Regan, 2007). And while the administration marketed itself on a pro-women agenda – appointing accomplished females to the president's inner circle and vowing to support women's rights in Afghanistan and Iraq while protecting ladies on the home front – Bush's "W Stands for Women" blustering rang untrue when it came to his policies, which have been described by feminists as anti-woman, or, to put it plainly, "stealth misogyny" (Ferguson and Marso, 2007: 1–3). American women faced a political landscape in which they were rhetorically supported but politically undermined. While it may seem silly to suggest that celebrity gossip magazines offered women a remedy to the politics of the Bush era, one can see how these publications, with their emphasis on female opinions and experiences, could seem especially appealing to women facing this troubled period in American history.

But what is perhaps most notable about W's vocally supportive yet functionally dismissive position toward women is that it is indicative of his administration's entire public relations strategy. During his time in office, the president received widespread national and international media coverage, much of which, according to *New York Times* columnist and author Frank Rich, was deeply influenced by the strong arm of Bush's public relations team, who encouraged exaggeration, speculation, and a thick PR gloss. In his 2006 book, Rich claims that the George W. Bush administration manipulated the American public, distracting us with false information, fear tactics, and stage-set public relations stunts designed and executed with the attention to detail typically reserved for the season finale of *The Apprentice* (2006: 172). The result was what Rich calls "the decline and fall of truth" in America.

Rich writes of what is, in his mind, the single most revealing paragraph anyone has reported about the Bush administration. Published in *The New York Times Magazine* in the weeks preceding the 2004 election, it recounts the condescending remarks made by a Bush aide who claimed that reality "is not the way the world works any more." "We are an empire now," the aide told author Ron Suskind. "When we act, we create our own reality" (Rich, 2006; 3). This snap-and-it's-true approach to veracity defined the Bush presidency, as evidenced by the May 2003 "Mission Accomplished" speech, delivered by President Bush from atop the USS *Abraham Lincoln* aircraft carrier. Two short months after deploying troops to Iraq under the auspices of destroying Saddam Hussein's weapons of mass destruction (WMDs), the United States military, we were told, had succeeded. But despite Bush's convincing costuming and patriotic set, "Mission Accomplished" turned out to be little more than performance. His blustering claim on success did little to mask growing skepticism about the war and its justifications. Today, after 10 years of conflict, troops remain in Iraq, the mission still not accomplished.

While mainstream news outlets struggled to make sense of (or, in some cases, simply regurgitated) the Bush rhetoric, political comedians Jon Stewart and Stephen Colbert earned high ratings and big laughs by parodying the news on their Comedy Central television shows. Americans, trying to understand the actions of an administration that seemed to say one thing and mean another, found relief in the hosts'

ability to lay bare the ever-growing array of political contradictions. In 2005, Colbert coined the term "truthiness,"
referring to a form of truth that a person claims to know
intuitively, emotionally, or "from the gut," without regard
for evidence or logic. The term quickly caught on. Named
"Word of the Year" by the American Dialect Society and
Merriam-Webster, "truthiness" has since been used and discussed in *The Washington Post*, *The New York Times*, CNN,
Salon, Nightline, and the Associated Press. "Truthiness is
tearing apart our country," Colbert argued in a 2006 interview with *The Onion*. "It used to be, everyone was entitled
to their own opinion, but not their own facts. But that's not
the case anymore. Facts matter not at all. Perception is everything. It's certainty."[5]

Celebrity gossip magazines became a part of the American
zeitgeist during a time when the notion of "truth" was being
seriously redefined within the country's socio-political arenas.
These magazines – which offer readers a world in which the
line between reality and public relations is ever-shifting and
in which the stories up for offer are almost always subject to
doubt, speculation, and opinion – resound with a readership
that has spent a decade wondering over the reliability of
politicians and journalists. But unlike mainstream news,
wherein the consequences of fabrication and misreporting are
matters of national security and liberty, celebrity news is low
stakes. That story about Taylor Swift's latest breakup *might
not* be true, but even if it's not, it won't start a war or get
someone killed. And in the meantime, it's a lot of fun to talk
about.

The notion of truthfulness, and ambiguous truthfulness in
particular, has been a resounding theme in twenty-first-
century American culture. Celebrity gossip magazines, with
their unnamed sources, penchant for hype, and notorious
fallibility resonate with a readership that has become highly
attuned to the question of truth. But these magazines offer
something different: a break from the confusing world of
mainstream news, a place where everything is open to interpretation, and female concerns are on the table. Here, truth
is up for grabs, available to be snatched up not by the politically connected but by the reader herself. Here, news
stories wear their ambiguity on their glittery sleeves, playfully

offering up opportunities for discussion and debate. This chapter examines the notion of truth in relation to celebrity gossip magazines, investigating the ways in which the genre's producers understand the concept of truth and the impact that the polysemic nature of these texts have on readers' ability to interpret the magazines in ways that are both personal and pleasurable.

Creating Truth: Editorialization and Authority

In 2007, *Us Weekly* began featuring an editorial segment entitled "All the News That's Fake," designed to call out competitors who had printed untrue, inaccurate, or misleading stories. *Advertising Age*, who winkingly called the allegations a "shocker!" reported that "if beauty is truth and truth beauty . . . then *Us Weekly* thinks it's pretty."[6] But *Us* was not the only publication with such illusions. While *Us* editor-in-chief, Janice Min, decried the celebrity magazine industry's willingness to accept "fiction," Bonnie Fuller, editorial director of *Star* magazine, had this to say to LXTV:

> *The New York Times* does not fact-check. Most newspapers do not fact-check. We not only fact-check, we have to have multiple sources on big stories. Everything is read. Every single thing is read – every caption, every article, by an in-house legal team – to make sure that we really do have it and that the sources are good sources. We take tremendous care with our work. We can't just put in things. If we are going to report rumors, we'll say, "This is a rumor we heard." But when we're reporting a story, we present you with what we've learned and it's been stood up by sources. We often get sources to sign legal agreements saying they'd go to court and attest to what they're saying is true.[7]

Across the industry, editors and publishers were speaking out, defending the credibility of the celebrity gossip genre. But were they schizophrenic? Delusional? How could they claim credibility when the stories they print, more often than not, turn out to be exaggerated or entirely fabricated?

While editors insist that celebrity news stories are cross-checked with a representative of the star involved and that, in order to gain legal approval, a piece of information must be confirmed by one, two, or three witnesses or sources, Rob DeMarco admits, "the genesis of some of these stories can be something very simple. A simple thing that's said or a nuance you pick up on. Those kinds of observations are in many ways what news, or speculative news, is about. It's really editorializing things more than straight reporting the news."

Celebrity gossip magazines are constantly involved in a process of translation and speculation, known in the industry as *editorialization*. This process involves a complex blend of data collection, interpretation, and opinion-formation. Each week, celebrity journalists consider a wide variety of informational cues in order to develop ideas for the upcoming issue. Details surrounding past events, quotes from the stars themselves, and even tidbits from a performer's film or music career can be molded into a new story. Through the process of editorialization, writers and editors act as translators, interpreting and communicating information to their readers in a way that transforms assumptions and opinions into news.

Take, for instance, a December 2009 story in *In Touch*, entitled "Is John Dissing Jessica and Jen?" The story speculates as to whether song lyrics written by pop star John Mayer contain coded messages about Mayer's past girlfriends, Jessica Simpson and Jennifer Aniston. Its opening paragraph reads:

> John Mayer is known for blabbing about his relationships to anyone who will listen, and now he's getting really personal in his songs on his new album *Battle Studies*. And many of the songs seem to be about his exes Jennifer Aniston and Jessica Simpson. "Sure, it's autobiographical," John, 32, told CNN.com. "Who would I be if I sat here and said that they're not about people or experiences I've had?" John admits he made the lyrics cryptic on purpose and challenges listeners to figure out who he's crooning about: "I say, 'Good on you, Sherlock Holmes!'" Hey, John, it's not that hard to decode!

Here, we see how an unremarkable comment by a pop musician is converted into an entire article, wherein the writer explicates the "true" meaning of Mayer's lyrics, using insider knowledge and the aforementioned sleuthing skills.

The article goes on to interpret ambiguous lyrics, such as "push it in and twist the knife again" and "why do you want to break my heart" as clear references to Simpson and Aniston. Photos and information about the two women and their relationship with Mayer appear alongside the lyrics, as further "evidence." In addition, a side panel, which proclaims "Jessica is sending a message to Tony, too!", features a picture of Simpson wearing a Dallas Cowboys hat and sweatshirt. From her choice of apparel, the writer infers that Jessica has not recovered from her relationship with quarterback Tony Romo, who "dumped" her five months previously.

This story makes the editorialization process explicit, demonstrating how it is that celebrity journalists cull together and decode information in order to create an original narrative. Furthermore, "Is John Dissing Jess and Jen?" models these decoding techniques for the reader, encouraging her to put on her sleuthing cap, connect the clues, and suss out her own theory of what John is *really* singing about. In doing so, this story, and others like it, equip readers with what Gamson calls "viewing tools," strategies that allow readers to "peel away the veneer" of the celebrity and thereby access the "real" star (1994: 48). The editorialization process not only allows the magazines to generate content and enhance their role as celebrity gatekeeper, but also provides readers with a feeling of authority, a sense that, with a keen eye, they too can figure out the "truth" about their favorite celebs.

Indeed, that well-trained eye is critical because so many of the clues provided by the magazines are visual ones. In case readers feel that the claims of celebrity "insiders," "friends," and publicists are unreliable, the magazines offer images as irrefutable proof, documentary evidence of stars' "real" feelings and actions. Still, these images are often quite ambiguous themselves. Photographs are often manipulated in ways that create a story where little news exists. Susanne Rieth explains that photo editors are responsible for seeking out images about which editorial inferences could be made. The smallest details of a photograph – a new ring on an actress's left hand, a slight bunching in the midsection of her sweater, a warm glance between co-stars – could all be transformed into a storyline. "Maybe there's something in it, maybe not," says Rob. Nevertheless:

> any observations that you can make editorially or any kind of conjuring of what you think is going on here [can become a story] . . . Did she do something with her hair? Her face? Her nose looks bigger. Her nose looks smaller. We're constantly looking for that stuff, all day long. We're looking for every one of those little things . . . We can make a proverbial mountain out of a molehill.

As Susanne and Rob's comments make clear, while a photograph may serve as a form of visual evidence, just *what* that image proves depends largely on the deductions of celebrity journalists.

Editors often strategically pair images with stories to which they are not related in order to produce the desired dramatic effect. Photographs of stars looking angry or distressed are used to enhance allegations of a feud or breakup, while images of gorgeous, smiling celebs are paired with stories about romance and success. At times, the images chosen have little, if anything, to do with the story at hand, but are carefully selected from a vast archive in order to convey an intended emotion. Three types of images repeatedly appear to bolster the credibility of the celebrity gossip narrative. I call these the glory, guilt, and grief shot.

Each shot embodies a specific set of characteristics, which makes it instantly recognizable as that particular image type. The glory shot, used to enhance a story about a celebrity's success or happiness, consists of a posed, sometimes professional photograph of the star looking her best, smiling, and making direct eye contact with the camera. Alternatively, the guilt shot, which typically accompanies stories about infidelity, backstabbing, or feuds, is a candid, paparazzi photograph of the stars caught off guard. In a guilt shot, celebrities appear tense, upset, or gloating – in short, they appear guilty, as though they have done something wrong. Often, the guilt shot consists of two images spliced together, implying a romantic relationship that may or may not actually exist. Finally, the grief shot is a candid photo of a star looking upset, flustered, or distraught; these types of images are used to convey a sense of despair, and are coupled with narratives in which a celebrity has experienced infidelity, abuse,

Figure 5.1 The glory shot, the guilt shot, the grief shot; *OK!*, October 5, 2009/ *Star*, February 23, 2009/ *Star*, February 9, 2009. Courtesy of American Media, Inc. All rights reserved. Reprinted by permission

addiction, or death. On their own, these photos provide very little information – indeed, it is often difficult to tell whether a star is upset or simply squinting, caught mid-sentence by an eager photographer – however, when paired with the genre's emotional narratives, these images become highly compelling "proof" of the stars' "true" actions and emotions.

Another type of visual manipulation that is standard within the industry is the image splice, wherein two distinct photos are edited in such a way so that they appear to be actually one and the same. This type of splicing is used to imply an interaction between celebrities, even when that interaction may have never occurred. Susanne explains that, for legal reasons, editors are careful to ensure that these types of composites are obviously faked; however, she notes, there are times when photos are edited in a way that is intentionally misleading:

> If they're going to actually fake it, they legally have to put "photo composite" written in little letters on the side. Of course, very few people might see those little letters that are there. When I was at *Star*, one magazine had bought the exclusive, first pictures of Brad and Angelina together and they were on the beach. This magazine had bought them for a lot of money; they probably paid like 100 grand or something. But *Star* made a fake picture of them on a beach, and they wrote "photo composite" on it.

Figure 5.2 *Us Weekly*, October 12, 2009. Courtesy of Wenner Media. All rights reserved. Reprinted by permission

In this instance, *Star*'s tactics helped the magazine to sell copies and avoid being one-upped by a competitor who had paid top dollar for exclusive image rights. More routinely, however, celebrity weekly magazines splice images in order to provide compelling, if misleading, visual proof of their claims.

Although editors intentionally alter these images to produce a specific visual and narrative effect, they do not attempt to hide these strategies from their readership. On the contrary, at times, the magazines explicitly draw readers' attention to these manipulative techniques. For example, an April 2009 issue of *Us Weekly* features an article by Lauren Schutte, entitled "Fake News," which claims to reveal instances in which its competitors have spun "tall tales." In it, Lauren alleges that *OK!* magazine used Photoshop to cut Suri Cruise and Shiloh Jolie-Pitt out of original photos and paste them together on a new background, in order to make it seem as though the celebrity kids were "best friends" on a "tea party" playdate. By revealing this technique, *Us* is not only staking a claim for its own validity, but is also explicitly alerting its readers to this strategy. Lauren claims to be making her readers more attuned to instances of editorialization that appear in *competing* magazines; however, in doing so, she also reveals techniques that appear across the genre, providing readers with viewing tools that will help them see through to the "real" story.

The Pleasure of Detection

The magazines' willingness to expose their own ambiguous inner workings invites readers to question the accuracy of the text. And once one element of the magazines' authority is called into question, others begin to topple in turn. If the story about Amanda Bynes's latest car crash, for example, is not true, then perhaps, readers can infer, all famous women are *not* really size two supermodels who have perfect boyfriends and children who never poop or cry. This ambiguity therefore allows readers to push back against and, at times, firmly reject the rigid moral guidelines and feminine stereotypes that gossip narratives set forth. As they question the magazines' authority, readers manage their own relationship to these "impossible standards," picking and choosing which elements they relate to and which they reject.

Thus, despite their professed commitment to Truth with a capital "T," celebrity gossip magazines are primarily invested in creating content that will spark interest and conversation amongst their readers. To achieve this, writers and editors rely not only on information, but on insinuation and interpretation, generating speculative and opinion-based stories. In admitting, even pointing to, their own fallibility, the magazines show how the editorialization process works while inviting readers to draw their own conclusions and stake their own claims. Ambiguity is therefore crucial to the celebrity gossip genre because it draws readers into a constant tug-of-war between truth and opinion, fact and fiction. Audiences become active participants, informed respondents who have the skills and savvy required to challenge the authority of the magazine. In other words, the ambiguous nature of the celebrity gossip text allows readers to experience what Roland Barthes calls the pleasure of play.

In his 1987 book, *Television Culture*, media scholar John Fiske outlines one of Barthes' key arguments about the characteristics, functions, and affordances of any text:

> Barthes (1977) suggests that the pleasure of creating a text out of a work involves playing with the text, and he exploits the full polysemy of "play" in his ideas. Firstly, he says, the text has "play" in it, like a door whose hinges are loose. This "play" is exploited by the reader who "plays" the text as a musician plays a score: s/he interprets it, activates it, giving it a living presence. In doing this, the reader plays a text as one plays a game: s/he voluntarily accepts the rules of the text in order to participate in the practice that those rules make possible and pleasurable; the practice is, of course, the production of meanings and identities. (1987: 230–1)

The *rule* of celebrity gossip magazines is that they claim to tell the truth, but in fact the stories they tell are part of a complex system of image production in which truth is ambiguous at best. In order to *play* the text, readers accept the magazines' tenuous claims on veracity while at the same time acknowledging the genre's fallibility. Readers of celebrity gossip magazines happily follow the rules, because, they find, the game is so much fun.

Is Beyoncé pregnant again? Will Kim Kardashian wed Kanye West? Readers don't necessarily believe that celebrity tabloids report the truth but they don't really mind if what they're reading is fake. Gamson notes that fans associate a sense of doubt with celebrity gossip, but points out that their incredulity is unproblematic, a non-issue. "The fact that 'most of it is not true,' that 'it can be interpreted in a million different ways,'" writes Gamson, "is acknowledged but irrelevant" (1994: 173–4). Indeed, this is also the case for the Cube readers, many of whom question the accuracy of the magazines but do not find this lack of truthfulness to be bothersome. Mary and Nikki explain:

Mary: My enjoyment isn't based on whether or not it's true. I probably wouldn't enjoy the magazines more if I knew they were true. While I say that I tend to believe the stories, I think they're all trash. Who knows?

Nikki: You know it's not real and you just enjoy that it's so fake and it's so outrageous that you're like, "Come on now." It's really not true.

For these readers, the ambiguous truthfulness of the magazines does not detract from, but in fact adds to, the pleasure of the reading experience. Truthfulness is a moot point. By presenting a world of ambiguity in which the line between information and fabrication is thin and ever changing, celebrity gossip magazines allow their readers to pick and choose which narrative elements they wish to subscribe to and which they wish to reject. "Players . . . enjo[y] the collective process of making their own meanings, choosing their own beliefs" and, as Gamson makes clear, "the celebrity text, *because* it makes visible and available its own encoding processes, is particularly suited to games of audience meaning creation" (1994: 183). It is not whether a story is truthful, but how easily and pleasurably it can be activated, that matters to readers.

Hermes likens this kind of textual play to puzzle solving. Just as one solving a jigsaw takes pleasure in sorting through and organizing the pieces, readers enjoy trying to figure out what is "really" happening in the lives of celebrities (1995: 125). Helena, a 21-year-old student and educator at the Cube, describes her own puzzle-solving strategies:

> I look more at the pictures and I try to find more of the stars' own quotes because a lot of times they have "a friend says this about this person." Well, I want their own quotes. I don't necessarily want "a friend says this about them" because there's an interpretation in there. So I'll look for a quote of her saying "I want to have a baby.". . . It's her own quote that is interesting. Not another person's interpretation of what's going on.

Helena has derived a set of specific strategies that she employs in an effort to puzzle out the truth of celebrity gossip. She uses direct quotations as a way of filtering away the editorial point of view contained in the magazines, thereby choosing for herself which narrative details she will and will not accept. For Helena and others, enjoyment of the reading experience is directly linked to an ability to puzzle solve.

The "fun" of celebrity gossip is that it allows, and even encourages, doubt and debate. But this opportunity for opposition is not only pleasurable, it is also a form of resistance, for the ambiguous nature of celebrity gossip magazines and their playability allows the Cube women to disagree with or reject the genre's messages. Because the magazines function as ambiguous texts, the task of interpretation is left up to the reader. Often, the Cube women express disbelief and dissention, contesting the magazines' claims, especially in regards to matters of appearance and behavior. Helena, Danielle, and Amber explain:

Helena: Sometimes it's fun to figure out if they *are* right . . . The [columnists] have their opinions intertwined. Sometimes one of them says her hair doesn't work with the dress or her shoes are completely off and you have to take your own opinion and say, "Well, I actually really like those shoes" or "Her hair looks really nice with that."

Danielle: I like debating. "No, I think that outfit looks *good*" or "No, he *is* a lying, cheating dog." It's just all in fun.

Amber: It's fun to disagree with them all the time. It's pure entertainment. It's not anything serious. That's another reason why it's fun for me.

These readers find "fun" in the simple act of disagreeing with the magazines' opinions on a hairstyle or dress. This pleasure is rooted in the reclamation of authority, however personal or insignificant that authority may initially appear. As they talk back to the text, the Cube women exert control over their reading experience in a way that is both empowering and enjoyable. By asserting their right to disagree, readers begin to scratch chinks into the magazines' authorial armor.

These chinks become deeper as debates over personal opinion evolve into discussions about femininity and female life. Because the Cube women do not only call the magazines' authority into question over matters of style; they also use the process of editorialization to "play" with the feminine norms that the magazines make so clearly available. Readers are especially eager to contest two normative models that are continuously rehashed within the genre: the thin ideal and the ideal of the heroic pregnancy. Here, Sasha, Helena, and Mary explain how they deal with instances in which they disagree with the magazines:

Sasha: There's times when I want to fling the thing across the room because I'm not in agreement! I've been known to say some unpleasant words about how I feel about what's written. Sure. It's your opinion so you have a right to voice and express it. It's about choice and variety and spice of life. "Oh, that girl looks like a scarecrow!" or "Oh no, that's a very unique, chic, edgy look!" You'll go back and forth, so yeah, it is fun [pitting] your opinion against what they feel because none of it is factual. Very little, if any [is true]. It is fun . . . Sometimes you get into a friendly, respectful debate over stuff. "No it isn't!" "Yes it is!" "I'll be damned! No it's not!" It *is* fun. I think it's designed to be fun. It's meant to be fun. Anybody that doesn't find it fun or at least humorous, they're taking it out of context.

Helena: You see all these perfect models, quote unquote perfect models, and it's really unfair because [I had a friend who] was really very upset about herself. She was trying to throw up and she was trying to eat less. She wouldn't eat anything! . . . And I kept telling her, "You're perfect, you're fine! There's nothing to worry about!" But she would say [pointing to the magazines] "but look at this, but look at this, look at her, she's gorgeous, look at the magazine, look, look, look!" And I said, "That doesn't matter, they could be computerized. They could go over that, they could airbrush it." "No, no, they look so pretty." "Well, that doesn't mean she actually looks that way." . . . You have to take everything in them with a grain of salt, basically. Basically weeding it out. You definitely have to take your own perspective.

Mary: I think when [the magazines] talk about how women lose the baby weight, what they're not saying is that their job is to lose the baby weight. And they have trainers and people cooking their meals for them and stylists and air-brushing and knowing how to dress properly. But also some of them have five, six hours a day to work out and they do, every day of the week. They have a nanny and a chef and a whole crew to help them whip their body back into shape. The magazines don't show that. They just say, "Look how great! Three months post-baby!" That's definitely misleading.

A lot of times you would see something like, "Party Girl Transformed." Bad photos, arrests, drunken flings, and then a comparison showing them talking about how [pregnant celebrities] just want to be home and how they feel they've changed and pictures of them knitting or something like that, something very subdued. I feel like they almost want to comfort people if a party girl gets pregnant. The world is going to be worried. No, no, it's OK. She's OK now. She's calm and a good mom. Which, I feel like a lot of times, is a huge scam . . . I mean, it's all how PR spins it.

These readers are aware, careful, and nuanced in their interpretations; their reading process is chock full of questions and doubts. Here, the authority lies not with the magazine, but with the readers who scrutinize and dissect the genre's claims, talking back to the so-called norms that it so ardently insists upon.

As they question, dispute, and even scoff at celebrity narratives, the Cube women challenge not only the magazine itself, but also the moral claims expressed throughout the text. In voicing their doubt and dissent, readers push back against the strictures on women's appearance, lifestyle, and attitudes that are so deeply engrained in gossip narratives. Here, knowledge of the editorialization process is crucial, for it is this knowledge that allows readers to justify their disagreement. Just as Helena and Mary point out the magazines' penchant for airbrushing and public relations, many of the Cube women reference the behind-the scenes mechanisms that allow celebrity gossip narratives to appear "real":

Helena: You hardly know anything. If you read a couple of articles on Jennifer Aniston, you feel like you know who she is and how she works and all that stuff. But you have to make sure to ground yourself again and say, "No, I really don't know this person because I am not getting their view. I am getting a processed view. This person took a picture but then other journalists take it and say this and take what she said and make a thousand interpretations of it."

Cynthia: Most of the times I don't believe what they print. I don't even believe the photographs. There are ways to alter things today. Where years ago where they would say, "Woah, we have a picture." You'd say, "OK." But now with all the ways there are today to alter photographs. If you look at a female's body in there or something. I don't believe any of it. Airbrushing and all that stuff.

Amber: You know nothing in there is true. *Star* . . . None of them are ever confirmed by whoever they're talking about. Nothing about their stories ever comes out to be true or admitted. I don't believe anything in most of these magazines. And that's another reason that I don't feel bad critiquing with the magazine because I know it's probably not true anyway.

As they highlight the ways in which the magazines fake it, the Cube women hold the genre's feminine standards up for inspection and find that there is, in fact, a man (or woman) behind the curtain of feminine perfection. The "normal" women who appear in these magazines are far from ordinary;

they are airbrushed, digitally manipulated and treated with a cool, crafted veneer. The version of femininity that is presented as obtainable is, in actuality, a facade, a myth, a fairy tale.

Readers take pleasure in the process of demystifying these powerful messages because in doing so, they not only assert their authority over the claims of the celebrity gossip magazine, they also resist the normative ideals of femininity that pervade their media environment and, indeed, much of contemporary American popular culture. Paradoxically, the genre's hyper-emphasis on feminine "norms" works to legitimize these ideals, but it also makes them available for public critique. On the one hand, many of the Cube readers report that they do, at times, feel vulnerable to the incessant messages about thinness, beauty, and motherhood; on the other hand, these same women enjoy picking apart these messages as they dissect the magazines' stories. The Cube women take great pleasure in engaging in these types of critiques. The opportunity to talk back is one of the key reasons why readers, even those who reject the genre's normative messages, find themselves plucking the latest issue of *In Touch* off the staff-room table or the supermarket shelf.

But let us not forget how it is that readers come to be aware of the inner workings of the celebrity gossip genre in the first place; the magazines themselves provide the insider knowledge, the viewing tools that allow audiences to engage in these negotiated readings. The magazines guide the reader, step by step, through the editorialization process, encouraging her to draw her own inferences and make her own conclusions. The magazines call attention to their own mechanisms, showing the reader how and when images are manipulated in service of a particular narrative. Furthermore, celebrity gossip calls upon the reader, invites her to become an active adjudicator in its moral universe. Polls directly address audience members, asking, "Who wore it better?" and "What do you think of the latest controversies?" Readers are encouraged to judge, rank, and comment on, to weigh in, to voice their concerns, to let their opinions be heard. "And with each question, betrayal, triumph, or crisis," Douglas notes, "judgment *is* required; it is a given that you are an authority on such matters and will bring your own social knowledge and moral compass to bear on the topic at hand" (2010: 249). Because the contents of the magazine are based largely on speculation, the reader's opinion is no more or less valid than the opinion set forth by the magazine, or by any other reader. The ambiguous truthfulness of the celebrity gossip magazine, therefore, produces it as a site of contestation and deliberation while simultaneously constructing its readers as active participants in an ongoing debate.

This is no happy accident. According to Rob DeMarco, the magazines are intentionally designed to encourage these types of self-directed, participatory engagements. Rob argues that celebrity journalists are not only *aware* that readers develop these types of interpretations, but that they actually compose stories in ways that *promote* these contested readings. "Our attitude is, let's give them the facts, let's show them the pictures, let's present it in a positive way or in a way that we're not looking judgmental and we'll let the readers decide what they think," says Rob, who is quick to point out that he and fellow staffers anticipate a reader response that is less than rosy. For example, stories about celebrity children often depict toddlers in high-fashion clothing, surrounded by mountains of luxury goods. These stories are framed in a positive light; their message is ostensibly, "Look at these cute, lucky kids!" But Rob and other staffers are aware of, and indeed promote, a second-level reading:

> We're sitting there going, "What a spoiled little brat this kid is!" but we don't want to say that. We don't want to say, "She's a spoiled little brat," so we're saying, "Here she is with all her stuff." But we want the readers to think, "Oh, what a spoiled little brat she is." And so we let the readers draw their own conclusions, which gets them involved in it to a certain extent. So it's intentionally done.

Celebrity journalists like Rob expect a reader response that directly contests the moral frame that they provide and intentionally craft their narratives in a way that allows readers to become "involved," to enjoy playing with those narratives.

"The pleasurable freedom of celebrity gossip" is, therefore, as Gamson argues, "built precisely on its freedom from but resemblance to truth" (1994: 177). In order to work as ambiguous texts, the magazines must appear authentic, credible, and ingenuous (Eco, 1978: 162). They must loudly maintain their commitment to truth for they cannot let the reader know that *they* know, *the reader* knows, it's all a game. The pleasure of play is possible if and only if the magazines present themselves as artless and unaffected; the magazines, therefore, loudly deny the fact that they are, in reality, complex and sophisticated texts designed to create a compelling and pleasurable experience for their readership.

"The power of play," writes Fiske, "involves the power to play with the boundary between the representation and the real, to insert oneself into the process of representation so that one is not subjected by it, but, conversely, is empowered by it" (1987: 236). For the Cube women, the pleasure of celebrity gossip magazine reading is that it affords them the power to challenge mass-mediated representations of femininity and female life. It would, however, be naive to suggest that all readers engage in these types of readings at all times or that the impossible standards produced and promoted by the magazines are negated by these sophisticated readings. They are not. Even those readers who challenge the text in certain contexts accept it at face value in others. Indeed, some of the Cube women report that their own tendency to agree or disagree with the magazines depends on their emotional state and motivation for reading; women who are experiencing personal hardship or who read as a way of "getting away from it all," for example, report that they are less likely to dispute the magazines' claims. But it would be equally false to suggest that celebrity gossip magazines are simply ideological booby traps designed to ensnare unsuspecting women. To argue thus is to ignore the pleasure that these texts afford their readers. Celebrity gossip magazines are complex texts, intentionally designed to allow readers to develop their own, polysemic interpretations. Whether or not their contents are true, whether that bulge really *is* a baby bump or simply an ill-positioned T-shirt, does not matter to readers because it is precisely this ambiguity that affords them the opportunity to consider and critique, to revel in and revolt against, both the magazine and the feminine "norms" it reproduces.

The power of play also reinforces the celebrity gossip magazine as a guilty pleasure. The magazines put feminine "norms" on display, splashed in bold-print neon, made impossible to ignore by the ubiquitous stars who smile and sob on their covers. In doing so, the genre makes these rigid standards of femininity, nebulously floating about in so much of the mass media, tangible, accessible, and refutable. Some of the Cube women feel guilty about purchasing and enjoying these texts, which perpetuate stereotypes that they, personally, reject. But celebrity gossip magazines are also designed to allow women, even those who abhor the "worst beach bodies" articles and the bump patrol, to revel in a fantasy world, a world in which those impossibly high standards of femininity are brought down to the level of ordinary life and thereby made accessible, manageable, and breakable. Thus, the magazines allow and, indeed, encourage women to confront and challenge contemporary culture's narrow, obsessive, and often troubling images of femininity.

This is the double-edged sword, the two-headed monster, the alluring cocktail of fun (with a splash of guilt) with which celebrity gossip magazines, and indeed all popular feminine texts, tempt their readers. The appeal of these texts lies in their ability to acknowledge and make plain the contradictory experience of being female. The love–hate relationship that women have with celebrity gossip magazines (and soap operas, and dating shows, and romance novels) is indicative not only of women's conflicted relationship with the media, but also of our complicated and contested relationship to contemporary discourses of femininity and to our contradictory place within patriarchy. Popular feminine texts allow female audiences, in a lighthearted and enjoyable way, to confront their contradictory relationship with normative femininity and to thereby exert authority over it. And while there is no guarantee that these moments of contention protect women from the powerful and often problematic messages that these texts present, the ability to question, challenge, and play remains an important affordance of the popular feminine, for it is through the power of play that women can, both individually and collectively, stake their claims against a web of competing discourses.

Conclusion

On Pleasure and the Popular

Since the start of the new millennium, celebrity gossip magazines have taken their glossy, garish place at the forefront of American popular culture. Their success has come at a time when the publishing industry at large has suffered enormous blows due to the economic recession and the increased availability of online content. Newspaper sales have dropped along with magazine subscriptions and advertiser spending on print (Farhi, 2006; Ives, 2009). But while some have worried that the celebrity weekly market is oversaturated and doomed to fail – in 2007 *Advertising Age* predicted that the magazines were "maxing out,"[1] – the genre's continued growth has thus far been a relative success in a dismal market, especially compared to other female-oriented publications, whose ad revenues have been steadily declining (Magazine Monitor, 2008).

Us Weekly's circulation has consistently expanded over the past 10 years – circulation was up 112 percent between 2001 and 2010 – and sales continue to trend upward, despite precarious market conditions.[2] Across other publications within the genre, sales have remained generally consistent, with only slight gains or losses. *In Touch*, for example, has retained a readership of approximately 7.6 million since 2009; meanwhile sister publication *Life & Style* added around 250,000 readers to its ratebase of 450,000 between 2009 and 2011.[3]

And while *Star*'s readership has dropped nearly 50,000 since 2008, it continues to reach over 10 million readers each week, with sales up 38 percent since its conversion from a paper tabloid.[4]

But despite their success thus far, the magazines are increasingly linked to and in competition with digital celebrity content. Countless blogs, websites, Twitter accounts, Tumblrs, YouTube channels, and Facebook pages have emerged in the wake of the celebrity gossip genre. PerezHilton.com, TMZ (website and television show), and X17 online all debuted between 2005 and 2007, bringing star gazing, snarky commentary, and access to the latest paparazzi photos straight to computer screens across the country and around the globe. For those working in print, online competition prompts a need for differentiation. "The world moves so fast," explains *OK!*'s Valerie Nome. "It's crazy. It's constant. Online is up-to-the-minute but when you open the magazine [it] offers an experience." And certainly celebrity gossip magazines do, as this book has shown, offer a specific reading experience. It may, however, be useful to consider the relationship between print and digital media as a symbiotic, rather than antagonistic, one, since even the magazines themselves have their own websites.

Many of the Cube women report engaging with celebrity content in both digital and print formats, and conversations amongst readers include information gleaned from a variety of sources. Further, as Meyers writes, because gossip blogs lie outside of the machinery of celebrity production and therefore have little stake in upholding the aura of the star, online content tends to traffic in a catty, game-like form of gossip that is instantly accessible, highly interactive, and endlessly "share-able" (Meyers, 2012). Audiences' online engagement with narratives that may be irreverent or subversive may therefore impact their tendency and ability to question and critique similar narratives when encountered in print. As the digital media landscape continues to expand, and as print media evolves to respond to readers' changing expectations, additional research is needed to fully understand when and why audiences seek out these different formats. For the moment, it is clear that audiences are increasingly attending to celebrity narratives in multiple ways, many of which result in opportunities for conversation, sociable engagement, and critique.

Indeed, the experience of "sharing" that celebrity gossip magazines provide is also occurring digitally, as users Tweet, "like," post, and comment on the latest news and images. This type of digital engagement, like face-to-face gossip, allows audiences to connect with a community of fans and to share their ideas and opinions about celebrity content; however, digital sharing is often instant, anonymous, and free. Whether in print or online, celebrity narratives create opportunities for social engagement and gossip. Research has shown that gossip helps participants to establish and maintain relationships (Coates, 1989), manage anxieties around group norms (Jaworski and Coupland, 2005), and provide emotional support (Jones, 1980). The Cube readers report that gossip about celebrities allows them to benefit from *all* of these outcomes, creating an ongoing, deeply personal form of conversation and interaction that allows them to trade stories, develop friendships, and provide one another with emotional support. Further research is needed to determine how the interpersonal sharing facilitated by print media compares to that which occurs with the click of a mouse or the tap of a screen. What is clear is that gossip magazines are part of a broader network of celebrity texts, which are increasingly tied to emerging technologies, and that the practices readers employ when engaging these texts will likely be shaped by their encounters with digital celebrity content.

Working Through Gossip

Throughout this book, I have argued that celebrity narratives present their readers with contemporary fairy stories, and yet these stories are unlike traditional folktales in one crucial way. While ordinary fables inevitably reach a conclusion, celebrity gossip never ends. Readers get to see what happens after the princess gets married. Is everything *really* perfect? Does she *actually* get to live happily ever after? The answer is often "no." The story goes on. Life, with its ups and downs, goes on. The open-ended nature of the celebrity gossip genre leaves room for contestation, for speculation, and for the anticipation of seeing what comes next. There is always time for one more twist, one more chapter, one more moment to make the dream of happiness come true. For readers, this ensures an ongoing opportunity for engagement and excitement, a never-ending chance to question and play, while simultaneously working through one's own experiences and concerns.

The notion of *working through* is a Freudian one, which, in the clinical sense, describes the psychoanalytic process whereby patients repeatedly discuss the same topics as a way of uncovering and managing repressed emotions. This concept, however, can also be applied to the mass media, as John Ellis makes clear in his (2000) study of television. According to Ellis, "television imbues the present moment with meanings. It offers multiple stories and frameworks of explanation which enable understanding and, in the very multiplicity of those frameworks, it enables its viewers to work through the major public and private concerns of their society" (2000: 74). Gossip magazines perform a similar function for their readers, providing a constant stream of repetitive narrative content that allows for a continuous working through of difficult topics.[5] In addition, within these narratives readers also come to know celebrity "characters," who are, like themselves, working through the challenges and emotional realities of a particular life stage.[6] Combined with the predictability and uniformity of the genre, these features provide readers with an opportunity to work through – to consider, talk over, and come to terms with – the anxieties and difficulties facing women today. This opportunity to work through life challenges alongside other women is an element of celebrity magazine reading that the Cube readers find particularly cathartic.

That is not to say, however, that celebrity gossip magazines offer women a solution to their problems. Nor do they do seek to progressively affect the institutional structures and popular discourses that work to perpetuate unrealistic representations of femininity, even while they allow their readers to talk back to these representations. The enunciative productivity, the opportunity for resistance, that the texts provide is, therefore, as Fiske points out, limited to the moment in which it occurs and does not typically result in real social change (Fiske, 1992: 38). Further, readers who engage in celebrity bashing appreciate the chance to express themselves "in an environment where their anger will be understood and expected," but do not believe that their discussions will have a lasting impact (Jones, 1980: 197). Indeed, the Cube readers take pleasure in complaining about the magazines and their depictions, but also express a sense of disappointment in the brevity of their conversations and the fact that, despite their discussions, images of femininity in popular culture remain largely idealized and stereotyped.

Does the conversation generated by celebrity gossip magazines, then, matter at all? Even if it does allow women to publicly air their private worries and grievances, what is the impact of this dialogue if it does not seek to address institutional or political structures of power? We might dismiss celebrity gossip magazines, and other popular feminine texts, for their inability to affect tangible or lasting social change; however, to do so would be to ignore the ways in which these texts provide their readers with an opportunity to confront and work through – for as long as they need to, on their own terms, and in a way that does not take itself too seriously – their own identities, relationships, and desires.

The study of celebrity gossip magazines, like the study of romance novels, soap operas, women's magazines, "chick flicks," and talk shows that have come before it, shows us that the pleasures offered up by popular feminine texts are not false pleasures. Although we should acknowledge the ways in which the popular feminine reflects and re-produces images of women that are often heterosexist, exclusionary, and demeaning, we can also see how these texts afford their audiences important opportunities for engagement, conversation, and reflection. And while it would be wrong to sweep all women's experiences into a single category, it is equally imprudent to deny the fact that many women find solace, recognition, and, indeed, pleasure in the popular feminine. As Modleski writes:

> [the] enormous and continuing popularity [of popular feminine texts] . . . suggests that they speak to very real problems and tensions in women's lives. The narrative strategies which have evolved for smoothing over these tensions can tell us much about how women

have managed not only to live in oppressive circumstances but to invest their situations with some degree of dignity. (1982: 14–15)

Celebrity gossip magazines remain deeply contradictory texts, at once highly enjoyable and incredibly frustrating to their readers. As with all popular feminine texts, some might argue that their stereotyped representations of femininity outweigh their potential value, that women should turn off *The Bachelor*, burn their copy of *The Notebook*, and fling the latest issue of *Elle* into the trash. But what good would that do? Would it help us to achieve a brighter future? Or simply eliminate the hope for pleasure in the present? Ang writes:

> It is impossible to live solely with a feeling of discomfort. We cannot wait until the distant Utopia is finally achieved: here and now we must be able to enjoy life – if only to survive. In other words, any uneasiness with the present, with the social situation in which we now find ourselves, must be coupled with an (at least partial) positive acceptance and affirmation of the present. Life must be experienced as being worth the effort, not just because a prospect exists for a better future, but also because the present itself is a powerful source of pleasure. (1985: 133–4)

I suspect that the Cube women are not unique in their "uneasiness" with the moral codes that celebrity magazines traffic in, nor alone in their use of gossip as a way of simply getting through the day, sociably engaging with friends and family, relieving stress, or boosting their spirits. While it is true that celebrity gossip magazines, and similar popular feminine texts, do not overtly advance feminist goals or herald a political awakening, Ang's comments remind us that the purpose of the popular is not always to encourage resistance, but to help us find joy in our day-to-day lives. That, in and of itself, is valuable.

Does the pleasure women find in their ambiguous relationships with the magazines, or with the popular feminine writ large, outweigh their frustration with the genre's normative messages? Or do the pernicious stereotypes that are often deeply woven into these texts continue to perpetuate low self-esteem and cynicism, despite audiences' nuanced and contested readings? I still cannot say. Nor do I believe that the answer will ever be fixed or clear. Nevertheless, I hope that this book begins to show that celebrity gossip magazines are complex worlds which both reflect and shape our aspirations and points of view, providing real and meaningful pleasure while also inciting critique. And I hope that the fact that questions remain unanswered will encourage others to look closely at these texts and what they offer.

Despite their "trashy" reputation, popular feminine texts are more than just mindless indulgences; they represent for their audiences an important opportunity for expression, companionship, and dissent. They serve as a discursive space in which the deeply contradictory nature of femininity and female life is acknowledged, valued, and made available for public discussion. Popular feminine texts presume and produce an ever-linked female community of participants, providing their audience with a sense of connectivity and camaraderie while encouraging face-to-face conversations between peers and friends. As audiences balance their frustration with the present and their hopes for the future, they may raise an eyebrow, they may reconnect with a friend, they may laugh out loud. In this way, the popular feminine plays a crucial role in helping female audiences to manage the challenges of everyday life.

Appendix A: Reader Profiles

Amber is a 27-year-old, African-American college student who has been working in the guest services division of the Cube for seven years. Hailing from suburban New York, she enjoys listening to music, traveling, and spending time with her boyfriend and friends. Amber reads celebrity gossip magazines about five times each week.

April is a 26-year-old, Caucasian supervisor at the Cube. Having earned her Associate's degree, April also works in the healthcare industry and reads celebrity gossip magazines three times a week.

Cynthia is an Italian-American manager at the Cube. She is a divorced, proud mother of three who discusses celebrity gossip on a weekly basis.

Danielle is a 33-year-old Cube director of West Indian descent who reads the magazines three to four times per week.

Helena is a 21-year-old, Caucasian Cube employee and student. Having earned her Associate's degree, Helena is currently completing work toward a Bachelor's degree in psychology. She reads celebrity gossip magazines three times a week.

Lisa is a 30-year-old Caucasian woman who has recently become engaged to be married and reads celebrity gossip magazines in her spare time.

Mary is a 33-year-old manager at the Cube. She has earned both her BA and Master's degrees and currently lives with her boyfriend in suburban New York. Although Mary only reads the magazines once a week, she discusses celebrity gossip with friends and coworkers on a daily basis.

Nikki is a 28-year-old, Hispanic student of language, literature, and culture who discusses celebrity gossip with her friends and coworkers daily.

Sasha, an African-American woman who declined to reveal her age, describes herself as an avid reader and animal lover. Having earned her Bachelor's degree, she now works as an educator at the Cube museum and says she reads celebrity gossip magazines "any chance I get!"

Stacey is a 37-year-old, Italian-American lead-educator and program coordinator at the Cube. Stacey has earned a BA and Master's degree and reads gossip magazines about twice a week.

Stephanie is a 33-year-old African-American mother of three, who has been happily married for 12 years. In addition to her work as an executive assistant at the Cube, she also owns her own business in the creative arts. Stephanie engages in discussions about celebrity gossip about three or four times each week.

Appendix B: Editor Profiles

Rob DeMarco is the former senior photo editor of *Life & Style* magazine. Rob has worked in the photo industry for the past three decades, holding positions at *U.S. News and World Report*, *National Geographic*, *The New York Post*, and *Star* magazine. He has also served as the editorial director for TimePix. Rob currently works as an acquisitions editor for Q Editorial Services and Corbis.

Sarah Grossbart earned a degree in journalism from Michigan State University in 2004. She became an editorial assistant at *Us Weekly* after having worked as an intern and staff assistant at the magazine and now serves as a staff writer.

Valerie Nome is a self-proclaimed fan. She developed an early interest in celebrity culture and, after auditioning for the Mickey Mouse Club at age 12, decided to pursue journalism. A native of Ohio, she worked for the *Cleveland Plain Dealer* and the *Akron Weekly Journal* while earning a degree in journalism from Kent State. After college, Valerie took a job at MTV where, in 1998, she became the first person at the station to publish a full-length interview with Britney Spears. Valerie has since worked for *USA Today*, *Us Weekly*, *Entertainment Weekly*, and *Cosmo Girl*. She has been the celebrity editor for *OK!* magazine since 2005.

Susanne Rieth grew up in Queens and Brooklyn and graduated from New York's Pratt Institute in 2003. She served as photo editor at *Star* magazine from 2004 until 2007, before transitioning to work at *Life & Style*. She is currently an editor at *OK!*

Lauren Schutte, who hails from Texas, earned a degree in journalism from the University of Missouri in 2005 and, in 2007, was hired as assistant to *Us Weekly*'s editor-in-chief, Janice Min. The following year, Lauren was promoted to assistant editor at *Us*. She has also served as assistant editor at *Bridal Guide* magazine, staff reporter at *The Hollywood Reporter*, and entertainment writer at *The Daily*. Lauren is a freelance writer for Yahoo! and NBC News.

Joy Wood is a writer and editor. She graduated from Vassar College in 2004 with a degree in English and subsequently began work as an editorial intern at *Us Weekly*. A Michigan native, Joy returned to the state to pursue an MFA in fiction at the University of Michigan, which she completed in 2008. Her stories have been published in *Glimmer Train*, *Black Warrior Review*, and *The Journal*. She is the recipient of fellowships and residencies from the Djerassi Resident Artists Program, the Edward F. Albee Foundation, the Santa Fe Art Institute, and The MacDowell Colony.

Appendix C: Content Analysis of Female Celebrities in Cover Stories by Age

November–December 2009

Name	Age at time of publication	Number of appearances	Issues
Jaycee Dugard	18	1	IT 12–7,
Kristen Stewart	19	8	LS 12–17; OK 11–12, 11–19, 11–16, 11–30, 12–17; S 11–19; Us 11–30
Amanda Arlauskas	20	1	IT 12–21
Taylor Swift	20	3	OK 11–12, 11–16; Us 11–19
Rihanna	21	3	IT 12–17; S 11–12; Us 11–16
Elizabeth Smart	22	2	IT 12–17, 12–14
Mischa Barton	23	1	S 12–21
Lindsay Lohan	23	1	Us 12–14
Lea Michele	23	1	OK 11–16
Audrina Patridge	24	1	OK 11–12
Kendra Wilkinson	24	7	IT 11–12, 12–21, 12–28; LS 12–28; OK 12–14, 12–28; Us 12–17
Khloe Kardashian	25	3	LS 11–30, 12–14; OK 11–16
Molly Malaney	25	1	Us 11–19

Name	Age at time of publication	Number of appearances	Issues
Ashlee Simpson	25	1	Us 11–16
Kate Bosworth	26	1	S 11–16
Melissa Rycroft	26	3	IT 12–28; Us 11–19, 12–28
Carrie Underwood	26	1	Us 12–21
Jessica Biel	27	1	S 11–12
Leann Rimes	27	1	LS 11–16
Britney Spears	27	6	LS 11–12, 11–16, 12–14; OK 12–17; S 12–17, 12–14
Jodie Sweetin	27	1	S 11–12
Jessica Alba	28	1	Us 12–14
Beyoncé Knowles	28	1	IT 12–17
Nicole Richie	28	1	S 11–12
Ivanka Trump	28	4	IT 11–19; LS 11–19; OK 11–19; Us 11–19
Kim Kardashian	29	3	LS 11–12, 11–30; S 11–30
Minka Kelly	29	1	S 12–17
Elin Nordegren	29	5	OK 12–28; S 12–17; Us 12–14, 12–21, 12–28
Jessica Simpson	29	6	IT 12–28; OK 11–9, 12–14; S 11–19, 12–28; Us 11–16
Kate Hudson	30	1	LS 12–28
Kourtney Kardashian	30	5	IT 12–28; LS 11–16, 11–30, 12–28; OK 12–28
Katie Holmes	31	9	IT 11–12, 11–19, 11–16, 12–17; OK 12–17, 12–14; S 11–19, 11–30; Us 11–30
Kim Zolciak	31	1	IT 11–16
Alexis Bellino	32	1	S 11–30
Reese Witherspoon	33	2	Us 12–14, 12–28
Fergie	34	3	IT 11–16; LS 11–16; Us 11–16

Name	Age at time of publication	Number of appearances	Issues
Kate Gosselin	34	1	S 11–12
Angelina Jolie	34	15	IT 11–12, 11–16, 12–17, 12–14, 12–28; LS 11–12, 12–17, 12–28; OK 11–16, 12–28; S 11–16, 12–14, 12–28; Us 11–30, 12–17
Abby Rike	34	1	LS 11–19
Rachel Uchitel	34	3	IT 12–21; OK 12–21; S 12–21
Heidi Klum	36	1	Us 12–14
Tori Spelling	36	2	LS 12–21; S 12–17
Nicole Eggert	37	1	S 12–17
Gwyneth Paltrow	37	1	S 11–16,
Shauna Sand	38	1	S 12–17
Mariah Carey	39	1	S 12–17
Jennifer Aniston	40	7	IT 11–12, 11–19, 11–30; OK 11–12; S 11–19, 11–30, 12–21
Jennifer Lopez	40	1	IT 11–30
Celine Dion	41	1	LS 11–30
Lisa Marie Presley	41	1	S 11–19
Nicole Kidman	42	1	OK 12–14
Cindy Crawford	43	1	LS 11–30
Sandra Bullock	45	1	LS 12–21
Sarah Palin	45	1	IT 11–30
Vicki Gunvalson	47	1	LS 12–17
Oprah Winfrey	55	3	IT 11–30; LS 12–17; OK 12–17
39 Issues from November to December	IT = *In Touch* LS = *Life & Style* OK = *OK!* S = *Star* Us = *Us Weekly* Appearance = First or last name + photo on cover		

Notes

Introduction: Celebrity Gossip Magazines in American Popular Culture

1 Kerwin, A. (2000). Bet is set for *Us Weekly* as showtime approaches. *Advertising Age*, 71(11): 3–22.
2 Carr, D. and Manly, L. (2002, February 27). Editor coming to *Us Weekly* may turn up the sex and glitter. *The New York Times*, C1.
3 Ibid.
4 Traster, T. (2007). 100 most influential women: Bonnie Fuller, celebrity gossip's godmother. *Crain's New York Business*, 23(40): W16.
5 Carr, D. (2003, August 4). Gossip goes glossy and loses its stigma. *The New York Times*, pp. 1E.
6 Ibid.
7 Fine, J. (2003a). *Us Weekly*, *Yoga Journal* saw circulation soar in 2002. *Advertising Age*, 74(8): 16.
8 Granatstein, L. (2004a). *Star's* studded debut. *MediaWeek*, 14(2): 24–5.
9 Fine, J. (2003b). Fuller faces fresh hurdles as she enters world of tabs. *Advertising Age*, 74(30): 4–29.
10 Author unknown. (2004). Bauer can't get enough of celebrities. *MediaWeek*, 14(19): 58.
11 Fine, J. (2004). Magazine of the year: *Us Weekly*. *Advertising Age*, 75(43): S1–S12.
12 Ives, N. (2007b). Shocker! *Us* claims rivals lied to readers. *Advertising Age*, 78(19): 3–42.

13   Fine, J. (2004). Magazine of the year: *Us Weekly*. *Advertising Age*, 75(43): S1–S12.
14   Also see Lusted, D. (1991), who argues that television necessarily produces a "glut" of personalities.
15   The fact that these texts are not considered valuable enough to be included in library collections is indicative of the presumed lack of socio-cultural import of these publications and of popular culture, particularly women's popular culture, writ large.
16   MediaMark Research & Intelligence (MRI) Publisher's Statement: Fall 2008, Fall 2009.

Chapter 1   Gendering Celebrity Gossip

1   Colford, P. D. (2003, June 27). Bonnie Fuller bolts *Us* to join tabloids, *Daily News* (New York), Business, 74.
2   Fine, J. (2002, October 21). Editor of the year. *Advertising Age*, 73(42): S3, S10.
3   Joke Hermes (1995) finds that, for gay men, there may be some possibility of escaping the negative associations of the popular feminine by engaging in camp and ironic readings. I have also found this in my own anecdotal experience; however, this is an area that requires additional research.
4   At: <http://www.scribblingwomen.org/intro.html>.
5   MRI, 2010.
6   MRI, Fall 2012.

Chapter 2   All About Us: Celebrity Gossip Magazines and the Female Reader

1   MRI, Fall 2012.
2   Ibid.
3   MRI, Fall 2009.
4   The United States Census Bureau defines a metropolitan core-based area as a metropolitan area combined with surrounding communities that are highly economically and socially integrated into that core area. Retrieved from <www.census.gov /www/metroareas>.
5   In 2010, 69 percent of *Us Weekly* readers (compared to only 56.1 percent of all Americans) had some college education. MRI Doublebase 2009; 2010 United States Census; <www .census.gov>; <http://www.census.gov/hhes/socdemo/education /data/cps/2010/tables.html>.

6   Since beginning this study in 2009, the age of the average celebrity gossip magazine reader has risen from 32 to 35 and, overall, older women are reading the magazines at a greater rate. This shift may reflect the fact that women who began reading the magazines when they were younger have remained loyal fans; it may also reflect the fact that American women are waiting longer to get married and start families; <http://www.census.gov>.

7   I was unable to review the editorial calendar for *OK!* magazine.

8   Newman, J. (2005, March 14). Cover girl. *Brandweek*, 46(11): SR8–SR12.

9   Ives, N. (2008). How much for that baby on the cover? *Advertising Age*, 79(7): 3–22.

10   Howe, P. (2005). *Paparazzi*. New York: Artisan.

11   Newman, J. (2005, March 14). Cover girl. *Brandweek*, 46(11): SR8–SR12.

12   See Radway (1984) for a discussion of how romance novels provide readers with a similar experience.

13   See Appendix C for a more detailed breakdown of the data from this figure.

14   *Life & Style*, August 10, 2009.

15   See Meyers, K. (2012) for a discussion of visual proof and baby bumps.

16   This is a similar sense of connection and camaraderie that Berlant (2008) attributes to women's participation in the intimate public.

Chapter 3   Stars on Earth: The Paradox of Ordinary Celebrity

1   See P. David Marshall (1997) for a discussion of the semiotic value of celebrity and Hamilton, P. and Hargreaves, R. (2001) for a discussion of the relationship between celebrity, value, and photography.

2   Turner, J., and Banks, C. L. (2007). *Paris Hilton Inc.: The Selling of Celebrity*. [Motion picture]. Canada: CBC.

3   See: <www.okmagazine.com/about>; retrieved April 22, 2010.

4   Christie, A. (1962). *The Mirror Crack'd*. New York, NY: Pocket Books, p. 180.

5   Berlant's discussion of the intimate public also resonates with this idea of the intimate common world described by Hermes. See Berlant, L. (2008, pp. viii–ix).

Chapter 4   Making Morality Meaningful

1   As Lang (2012) makes clear, there is a notable distinction between how men and women are treated in the popular press when it comes to infidelity. The older, married director whom Stewart allegedly cheated with was largely ignored, while Stewart became the subject of a public attack. Similarly, when it was revealed in 2013 that Simon Cowell impregnated his best friend's wife, he was not subject to the kind of scrutiny endured by Stewart, but rather appeared on a variety of talk shows to discuss the news. In short, there exists a clear double standard in the moral codes of sexuality for men and women and the repercussions for those who fail to adhere to those codes are often deeply shaped by the gender of the actor.

2   See: <http://www.cdc.gov/nchs/data/nvsr/nvsr61/nvsr61_01 .pdf#table01>.

3   Since most celebrities are extremely wealthy, the financial underpinnings of heroic motherhood are typically unmarked, but taken for granted. Heroic mothers are often presented alongside beautiful nurseries or at baby showers heaped with luxurious gifts. Finances are only explicitly discussed when they become problematic. The most obvious example of this is in the case of Nadia Suleman, i.e., "Octomom," a single mother who was condemned in the tabloid press for her decision to have octuplets. Suleman was portrayed as the ultimate failed mother, in large part because she was unable to financially care for the newborns.

Chapter 5   Ambiguously Truthful

1   See: <http://www.fec.gov/pubrec/2000presgeresults.htm>.

2   Fine, J. (2003a, February 24). *Us Weekly, Yoga Journal* saw circulation soar in 2002. *Advertising Age*, 74(8): 16 (2/3p).

3   LXTV Interview [Video File]; retrieved from: <http://lxtv.com /lxoriginals/video/8412>.

4   Fine, J. (2004). Magazine of the year: *Us Weekly. Advertising Age*, 75(43): S1–S12.

5   Rabin, N. (2006, January 25). *Interview: Stephen Colbert*. A.V. Club. See: <http://www.avclub.com/articles/stephen -colbert,13970/>.

6   Ives, N. (2007b, May 7). Shocker! *Us* claims rivals lied to readers. *Advertising Age*, 78(19): 3–42 (2p).

7 LXTV Interview [Video File]; retrieved from: <http://lxtv.com/lxoriginals/video/8412>.

Conclusion: On Pleasure and the Popular

1 Ives, N. (2007a, April 9). Guess who's not getting any fatter! Celeb mags max out. *Advertising Age*, 78(15): 1–44, 2p.
2 ABC Publisher's Statements, December 2001–2010.
3 MRI, Fall 2009, Spring 2011.
4 MRI, Fall 2008, base adults.
5 Also see Bonner and McKay (2007) for a discussion of the concept of "working through" in relation to human-interest stories.
6 See Draper and Lotz (2012) for a discussion of the relationship between character development and "working through."

References

Aldridge, M. (2001). "Confessional culture, masculinity and emotional work," *Journalism*, 2(1): 91–108.

Ang, I. (1985). *Watching Dallas: Soap Opera and the Melodramatic Imagination*. London: Methuen.

Author unknown. (2004). Bauer can't get enough of celebrities. *MediaWeek*, 14(19): 58.

Ballaster, R., Beetham, M., Frazer, E., and Hebron, S. (1991). *Women's Worlds: Ideology, Femininity and the Woman's Magazine*. London: Macmillan.

Barrett, M. (1982). Feminism and the definition of cultural politics. In R. Brunt and C. Rowan (eds), *Feminism, Culture, and Politics*. London: Lawrence & Wishart.

Barthes, R. (1977). "From work to text." In R. Barthes, *Image-Music-Text*. London: Fontana, pp. 155–64.

Becker, K. (2008). Photojournalism and the tabloid press. In A. Biressi and H. Nunn (eds), *The Tabloid Culture Reader*. Maidenhead: McGraw-Hill/Open University Press, pp. 81–97.

Berlant, L. (2008). *The Female Complaint: The Unfinished Business of Sentimentality in American Culture*. Durham, NC: Duke University Press.

Bird, D. A. (1976). A theory for folklore in mass media: Traditional patterns in the mass media. *Southern Folklore Quarterly*, 40: 285–305.

Bonner, F., and McKay, S. (2007). Personalizing current affairs without becoming tabloid: The case of Australian Story. *Journalism: Theory, Practice and Criticism*, 8(6): 640–56.

Braudy, L. (1986). *The Frenzy of Renown: Fame and Its History*. New York: Oxford University Press.

Brewer, R. (2009). The "goss" on Paul and Heather: Attitudes to celebrity and divorce in three NZ women's magazines. *Pacific Journalism Review*, 15(1): 169–85.

Brown, M. E. (1989). Soap opera and women's culture: Politics and the popular. In K. Carter and C. Spitzack (eds), *Doing Research on Women's Communication: Perspectives on Theory and Method*. Norwood, NJ: Ablex Publishing Co., pp. 161–90.

Brown, M. E. (1990). Motley moments: Soap operas, carnival, gossip and the power of the utterance. In M. E. Brown (ed.), *Television and Women's Popular Culture: The Politics of the Popular*. Newbury Park, CA. Sage, pp. 183–98.

Brunsdon, C. (1978). *Everyday Television – Nationwide*. London: BFI.

Brunsdon, C. (2000). *The Feminist, the Housewife, and the Soap Opera*. Oxford: Oxford University Press.

Campbell, R., Martin, C. R., and Fabos, B. (2013). *Media and Culture: An Introduction to Mass Communication*. Boston: Bedford/St Martin's.

Carr, D. (2003, August 4). Gossip goes glossy and loses its stigma. *The New York Times*, E1.

Carr, D., and Manly, L. (2002, February 27). Editor coming to *Us Weekly* may turn up the sex and glitter. *The New York Times*, C1.

Cashmore, E. (2006). *Celebrity/Culture*. London: Routledge.

Chancey, J. R. (1999). Diana doubled: The fairytale princess and the photographer. *Feminist Formations*, 11(2): 163–75.

Christie, A. (1962). *The Mirror Crack'd*. New York, NY: Pocket Books.

Coates, J. (1989) Gossip revisited: Language in all-female groups. In Coates J. and Cameron D. (eds), *Women in Their Speech Communities: New Perspectives on Language and Sex*. New York: Longman, pp. 94–122.

Cohen, J. (2001). Defining identification: A theoretical look at the identification of audiences with media characters. *Mass Communication & Society*, 4: 245–64.

Colford, P. D. (2003, June 27). Bonnie Fuller bolts *Us* to join tabloids, *Daily News* (New York), Business, p. 74.

Connell, I. (1992). Personalities in the popular media. In P. Dahlgren and C. Sparks (eds), *Journalism and Popular Culture*. London: Sage, pp. 64–83.

Coward, R. (1985). *Female Desires: How They are Sought, Bought and Packaged*. New York: Grove Press, Inc.

D'Acci, J. (1994). *Defining women: Television and the case of Cagney and Lacey*. Chapel Hill, NC: University of North Carolina Press.

deCordova, R. (1990). *Picture Personalities: The Emergence of the Star System in America.* Chicago, IL: University of Illinois Press.

Dégh, L. (1994). *American Folklore and the Mass Media.* Bloomington, IN: Indiana University Press.

Deutsch, T. (2010). *Building a Housewife's Paradise: Gender, Politics, and American Grocery Stores in the Twentieth Century.* Chapel Hill, NC: University of North Carolina Press.

Douglas, S. J. (1994). *Where the Girls Are: Growing Up Female with the Mass Media.* New York: Times Books.

Douglas, S. J. (2010). *Enlightened Sexism: The Seductive Message that Feminism's Work is Done.* New York: Times Books.

Draper, J. and Lotz, A. D. (2012). "Working through" as ideological intervention: The case of homophobia in *Rescue Me. Television and New Media,* 13(6): 520–34.

Dumenco, S. and Kerwin, A. (2006). Shocker: Oprah pregnant with James Frey's baby! *Advertising Age,* 77(6): 46.

Dyer, R. (1991). *A Star is Born* and the construction of authenticity. In C. Gledhill (ed.), *Stardom: Industry of Desire.* London: Routledge, pp. 132–40.

Dyer, R. (1998). *Stars.* New edn. London: BFI Publishing.

Dyer, R. (2003). *Heavenly Bodies: Film Stars and Society.* 2nd edn. London: Routledge.

Eco, U. (1978). *The Role of the Reader: Explorations in the Semiotics of Texts.* Bloomington, IN: Indiana University Press.

Ellis, J. (2000). *Seeing Things: Television in the Age of Uncertainty.* London: I.B. Tauris.

Farhi, P. (2006). Under Siege. *American Journalism Review,* 28(1): 26–31.

Feasey, R. (2006). Get a famous body: Star styles and celebrity gossip in *heat* magazine. In S. Holmes and S. Redmond (eds), *Framing Celebrity: New Directions in Celebrity Culture.* New York: Routledge, pp. 177–94.

Feasey, R. (2008). Reading *heat*: The meanings and pleasures of star fashions and celebrity gossip. *Continuum: Journal of Media and Cultural Studies,* 22(5): 687–99.

Feilitzen, C., and Linne, O. (1975). Identifying with television characters. *Journal of Communication,* 25: 51–5.

Ferguson, M. (1983). *Forever Feminine: Women's Magazines and the Cult of Femininity.* London: Heinemann.

Ferguson, M. L., and Marso, L. J. (2007). Feminism, gender, and security in the Bush presidency. In M. L. Ferguson and L. J. Marso (eds), *W Stands for Women: How the George W. Bush Presidency Shaped a New Politics of Gender.* Durham, NC: Duke University Press, pp. 63–86.

Fine, J. (2002). Editor of the year. *Advertising Age,* 73(42): S3, S10.

Fine, J. (2003a). *Us Weekly, Yoga Journal* saw circulation soar in 2002. *Advertising Age*, 74(8): 16.

Fine, J. (2003b). Fuller faces fresh hurdles as she enters world of tabs. *Advertising Age*, 74(30): 4–29.

Fine, J. (2004) Magazine of the year: *Us Weekly*. *Advertising Age*, 75(43): S1–S12.

Fiske, J. (1987). *Television Culture*. London: Methuen.

Fiske, J. (1992). The cultural economy of fandom. In L. A. Lewis (ed.), *The Adoring Audience: Fan Culture and Popular Media*. London: Routledge, pp. 30–49.

Fraser, N. (1992). Rethinking the public sphere: A contribution to the critique of actually existing democracy. In C. Calhoun (ed.), *Habermas and the Public Sphere*. Cambridge, MA: MIT Press, pp. 109–42.

Friedan, B. (1963). *The Feminine Mystique*. New York: Norton.

Gamson, J. (1994). *Claims to Fame: Celebrity in Contemporary America*. Berkeley, CA: University of California Press.

Gill, R. (2007). Postfeminist media culture: Elements of a sensibility. European *Journal of Cultural Studies*, 10(2): 147–66.

Gluckman, M. (1963). Papers in honor of Melville J. Herskovits: Gossip and scandal. *Current Anthropology*, 4(3): 307–16.

Goffman, E. (1959). *The Presentation of Self in Everyday Life*. Garden City, NY: Doubleday.

Graham, H. (1976). The social image of pregnancy: Pregnancy as spirit possession. *Sociological Review*, 24: 291–308.

Granatstein, L. (2004a). *Star's* studded debut. *MediaWeek*, 14(2): 24–5.

Granatstein, L. (2004b). Captive audience. *MediaWeek*, 14(22): 32.

Green, M. C., Brock, T. C., and Kaufman, G. F. (2004). Understanding media enjoyment: The role of transportation into narrative worlds. *Communication Theory*, 14(4): 311–27.

Grindstaff, L. (2002). *The Money Shot: Trash, Class and the Making of TV Talk Shows*. Chicago, IL: University of Chicago Press.

Grossberg, L. (1992). Is there a fan in the house?: The affective sensibility of fandom. In L. A. Lewis (ed.), *The Adoring Audience: Fan Culture and Popular Media*. London: Routledge, pp. 50–65.

Gutterman, D. S., and Regan, D. (2007). Straight eye for the straight guy. In M. L. Ferguson and L. J. Marso (eds), *W Stands for Women: How the George W. Bush Presidency Shaped a New Politics of Gender*. Durham, NC: Duke University Press, pp. 63–86.

Habermas, J. ([1962] 1989). *The Structural Transformation of the Public Sphere: An Inquiry into a Category of Bourgeois Society*. Cambridge: Polity.

Hamilton, P., and Hargreaves, R. (2001). *The Beautiful and the Damned: The Creation of Identity in Nineteenth-Century Photography*. Hampshire, UK: Lund Humphries.

Hermes, J. (1995). *Reading Women's Magazines: An Analysis of Everyday Media Use*. Cambridge: Polity.

Herzog, H. (1941). On borrowed experience: An analysis of listening to daytime sketches. *Studies in Philosophy and Social Science*, 9(1): 65–95.

Hirschberg, L. (2010, November). The art of reality. *W Magazine*: 108–15.

Hobson, D. (1980). Housewives and the mass media. In S. Hall et al. (eds), *Culture, Media, Language*. London: Hutchinson, pp. 105–14.

Hobson, D. (1989). "Soap operas at work," In E. Seiter, H. Borchers, G. Kreutzner, and E. Warth (eds), *Remote Control: Television, Audiences and Cultural Power*. London: Routledge, pp. 150–67.

Hobson, D. (2003). *Soap Opera*. Cambridge: Polity.

Holmes, S. (2005). "Off-guard, unkempt, unready?" Deconstructing contemporary celebrity in *heat* magazine. *Continuum: Journal of Media and Cultural Studies*, 19(1): 21–38.

Holmes, S. (2006). It's a jungle out there!: Playing the game of fame in celebrity reality TV. In S. Holmes and S. Redmond (eds), *Framing Celebrity: New Directions in Celebrity Culture*. New York: Routledge, pp. 45–65.

Horton, D., and Wohl, R. R. (1956). Mass communication and para-social interaction: Observations on intimacy at a distance. *Psychiatry*, 19: 215–29.

Howe, P. (2005). *Paparazzi*. New York: Artisan.

Huyssen, A. (1986). *After the Great Divide: Modernism, Mass Culture, Postmodernism*. Bloomington, IN: Indiana University Press, pp. 44–62.

Ives, N. (2007a). Guess who's not getting any fatter! Celeb mags max out. *Advertising Age*, 78(15): 1–44.

Ives, N. (2007b). Shocker! *Us* claims rivals lied to readers. *Advertising Age*, 78(19): 3–42 (2p).

Ives, N. (2008). How much for that baby on the cover? *Advertising Age*, 79(7): 3–22.

Ives, N. (2009). Why ad pages won't ever fully return to mags. *Advertising Age*, 80(26): 3–20.

Jaworski, A. and Coupland, J. (2005). Othering in gossip: "You go out you have a laugh and you can pull yeah okay but like . . ." *Language in Society*, 34: 667–94.

João Silveirinha, M. (2007). Displacing the "political:" the "personal" in the media public sphere. *Feminist Media Studies*, 7(1): 65–79.

Johansson, S. (2006). "Sometimes you wanna hate celebrities": Tabloid readers and celebrity coverage. In S. Holmes and S. Redmond (eds), *Framing Celebrity: New Directions in Celebrity Culture*. New York: Routledge, pp. 343–58.

Johansson, S. (2007). "They just make sense": Tabloid newspapers as an alternative public sphere. In R. Butsch (ed.), *Media and Public Spheres*. New York: Palgrave, pp. 83–95.

Johnson, M. (2013, May 7). The gender coverup. *Huffington Post Books*. At: <http://www.huffingtonpost.com/maureen-johnson /gender-coverup_b_3231484.html>.

Jones, D. (1980). Gossip: Notes on women's oral culture. *Women's Studies International Quarterly*, 3: 193–8.

Katz, E. and Liebes, T. (1990). *The Export of Meaning: Cross-cultural Readings of Dallas*. Oxford: Oxford University Press.

Kerwin, A. (2000). Bet is set for *Us Weekly* as showtime approaches. *Advertising Age*, 71(11): 3–22.

King, S. (2001). *Magazine Design that Works: Secrets of Successful Magazine Design*. Gloucester: Rockport Publishers.

Kitch, C. (2009). Tears and trauma in the news. In B. Zelizer (ed.), *The Changing Faces of Journalism: Tabloidization, Technology and Truthiness*. London: Routledge, pp. 29–39.

Knee, A. (2006). Celebrity skins: The illicit textuality of the celebrity nude magazine. In S. Holmes and S. Redmond (eds), *Framing Celebrity: New Directions in Celebrity Culture*. New York: Routledge, pp. 161–76.

Lai, A. (2006). Glitter and grain: Aura and authenticity in the celebrity photographs of Juergen Teller. In S. Holmes and S. Redmond (eds), *Framing Celebrity: New Directions in Celebrity Culture*. New York: Routledge, pp. 215–30.

Lang, N. (2012, September 4). "Trampire": Why the public slut-shaming of Kristen Stewart matters for young women. *HuffingtonPost.com*. At: <http://www.huffingtonpost.com/nico-lang /trampires-why-the-slut-sh_b_1850940.html>.

Levin, J. and Arluke, A. (1987). *Gossip: The Inside Scoop*. New York: Plenum Press.

Lindlof, T. R., and Taylor, B. C. (2002). *Qualitative Communication Research Methods*. 2nd edn. Thousand Oaks, CA: Sage.

Lotz, A. (2007). *The Television Will Be Revolutionized*. New York: New York University Press.

Lusted, D. (1991). The glut of the personality. In C. Gledhill (ed.), *Stardom: Industry of Desire*. London: Routledge, pp. 251–8.

McCracken, E. (1993). *Decoding Women's Magazines: From Mademoiselle to Ms*. Basingstoke, UK: Macmillan.

MacKinnon, C. A. (1983). Feminism, Marxism, method, and the state: Toward feminist jurisprudence. *Signs: Journal of Women in Culture and Society*, 8(4): 635–58.

MacKinnon, C. A. (1989). *Toward a Feminist Theory of the State*. Cambridge, MA: Harvard University Press.

McLean, A. L. (1995). The Cinderella princess and the instrument of evil: Surveying the limits of female transgression in two post-war Hollywood scandals. *Cinema Journal*, 24(3): 36–56.

McRobbie, A. (1991). *Feminism and Youth Culture: From "Jackie" to "Just Seventeen"*. Basingstoke, UK: Macmillan.

Magazine Monitor (2008). *MediaWeek*, 18(30): 52.

Marshall, P. D. (1997). *Celebrity and Power: Fame in Contemporary Culture*. Minneapolis, MN: University of Minnesota Press.

Mayer, V., Banks, M. J., and Caldwell, J. T. (2009). Production studies: Roots and routes. In V. Mayer, M. J. Banks, and J. T. Caldwell (eds), *Production Studies: Cultural Studies of Media Industries*. London: Routledge, pp. 1–12.

Media Mark Research & Intelligence (MRI).

Merton, R. K., and Lowenthal, M. F. (1946). *Mass Persuasion: The Social Psychology of a War Bond Drive*. New York: Harper.

Meyers, E. (2012). Gossip blogs and "baby bumps": The new visual spectacle of female celebrity in gossip media. In K. Ross (ed.), *The Handbook of Gender, Sex, and Media*. Malden, MA: Wiley-Blackwell, pp. 53–70.

Meyrowitz, J. (1985). *No Sense of Place: The Impact of Electronic Media on Social Behavior*. New York: Oxford University Press.

Modleski, T. (1982). *Loving with a Vengeance. Mass-produced Fantasies for Women*. Hamden, CT: Archon Books.

Morley, D. (1986). *Family Television: Cultural Power and Domestic Leisure*. London: Comedia Pub. Group.

Nash, M. (2005). Oh baby, baby: (Un)veiling Britney Spears' pregnant body. *Michigan Feminist Studies*, 19: 27.

Negra, D. (2001). *Off-white Hollywood: American Culture and Ethnic Female Stardom*. London: Routledge.

Negra, D. (2009). *What a Girl Wants?: Fantasizing the Reclamation of Self in Postfeminism*. London: Routledge.

Newman, J. (2005, March 14). Cover Girl. *Brandweek*, 46(11): SR8–SR12.

Örnebring, H., and Jönsson, A. M. (2004). Tabloid journalism and the public sphere: A historical perspective on tabloid journalism. *Journalism Studies*, 5(3): 283–95.

Portmann, J. (2000). *When Bad Things Happen to Other People*. London: Routledge.

Rabin, N. (2006, January 25). *Interview: Stephen Colbert.* A.V. Club. Retrieved from: <http://www.avclub.com/articles/stephen -colbert,13970/>.

Radway, J. A. (1984/1991). *Reading the Romance: Women, Patriarchy, and Popular Literature.* Chapel Hill, NC: University of North Carolina Press.

Redmond, S. (2006). Intimate fame everywhere. In S. Holmes and S. Redmond (eds), *Framing Celebrity: New Directions in Celebrity Culture.* New York: Routledge, pp. 27–43.

Rich, F. (2006). *The Greatest Story Ever Sold: The Decline and Fall of Truth from 9/11 to Katrina.* New York: Penguin Press.

Rojek, C. (2001). *Celebrity.* London: Reaktion Books.

Rysman, A. R. (1977). Gossip and occupational ideology. *Journal of Communication,* 26: 64–8.

Scannell, P. (2007). *Media and Communication.* London: Sage.

Schudson, M. (1981). *Discovering the News: A Social History of American Newspapers.* New York: Basic Books.

Sternheimer, K. (2011). *Celebrity Culture and the American Dream: Stardom and Social Mobility.* London: Routledge.

Tebbutt, M. (1995) *Women's Talk?: A Social History of Gossip in Working-Class Neighborhoods, 1880–1960.* Brookfield, VT: Ashfield Publishing Co.

Traster, T. (2007). 100 most influential women: Bonnie Fuller, celebrity gossip's godmother. *Crain's New York Business,* 23(40): W16.

Tuchman, G. (1978). The symbolic annihilation of women by the mass media. In G. Tuchman, A. K. Daniels, and J. Benet (eds), *Hearth and Home: Images of Women in the Mass Media.* New York: Oxford University Press, pp. 3–38.

Turner, G. (2010). *Ordinary People and the Media: The Demotic Turn.* Los Angeles, CA: Sage.

Turner, J., and Banks, C. L. (2007). *Paris Hilton Inc.: The Selling of Celebrity.* [Motion picture]. Canada: CBC.

Walker, A. (1970). *Stardom: The Hollywood Phenomenon.* New York: Stein and Day.

Warwick, J. C. (2007). *Girl Groups, Girl Culture: Popular Music and Identity in the 1960s.* London: Routledge.

Williams, R. (1970). *The English Novel from Dickens to Lawrence.* New York: Oxford University Press.

Williamson, J. (1978). *Decoding Advertisements: Ideology and Meaning in Advertising.* London: Marion Boyars Publishers Ltd.

Winship, J. (1987). *Inside Women's Magazines.* London: Pandora Press.

Wolf, N. (1992). *The Beauty Myth: How Images of Beauty are Used Against Women.* New York: Anchor Books.

Index

act of reading, 13–14, 23, 84, 88, 90, 100
advertisements, 76–7
    ad sales, 2–3, 131
Advertising Age, 2–3, 25, 114, 131
al-Qaeda, 110–11
ambiguity, *see* truth
American Media, 3
Ang, Ien, 13–15, 35–9, 136
Aniston, Jennifer, 8, 62, 76–7, 82, 87, 100, 115–18, 126
authenticity, 5, 22, 68–74

baby bump, 1, 7–8, 62–3, 93–5, 129–30
Baskett, Kendra, *see* Kendra Wilkinson
Bauer Publishing, 3, 110–11
Berlant, Lauren, 30–1
blog, 3, 6, 32, 66–8, 132
body image, 7, 23, 42, 48–9, 93–8, 102–8, 125–6
Braudy, Leo, 5–6, 67
Brown, Mary Ellen, 38–9, 86
Bush, George W., 110–12

Carr, David, 2, 25
celebrity:
    industrial production of, 5, 69, 74
    paradox of the ordinary, 6, 22, 66–73
    participation with gossip press, 69–73
    typology of celebrity audiences, 15–16
celebrity bashing, 85, 101–4, 135
celebrity children, 70, 90, 120, 128
celebrity gossip magazines:
    definition of, 5
    design, *see* design
    female perspective, 7–8
    gatekeeping, 22, 74–9, 116
narratives:
    All the News That's Fake, 114
    analysis of narrative content, 48
    diets, 46, 49, 52, 82, 89
    domestic violence, 107–8

fashion, 48–9, 51–2, 77–8,
  89, 128
frequency of narratives,
  47–9
home tour, 78–9
Look for Less, 77–8
Love Lives, 45–6, 55
marriage, 7, 90–3
pregnancy, 47–8, 62,
  93–8
production schedule, 45
reporting, 46–7
celetoids, 6
circulation, 2, 110, 131
Colbert, Stephen, 112–13
conspicuous consumption,
  76–9, 92, 128
Cosmopolitan, 2, 26
cover, *see* design
critiques of popular culture:
  feminist, 10–13, 136
  ideology, 11–13, 37
  mass culture, 11–12, 28–9,
    35–8, 41
cultural studies, 12–14, 35

Dallas, 13–14, 39
deCordova, Richard, 4–6, 23,
  91
demotic turn, 68
design:
  arrows, 54, 62–3, 75, 94
  color, 2, 5, 50, 53–64
  cover, 50, 53–4, 60–1
  direct address, 23, 63, 82
  first names, 54, 76–7, 82
  organization, 54–5
  personal pronouns, 61–2,
    77, 82
  photographs, 54–9
  predictability, 50–4, 134
diversity, 99–100
Douglas, Susan, 7, 10–12, 37,
  43, 62, 77, 89, 98, 111,
  127–8

Dyer, Richard, 6, 72, 87,
  93
Eco, Umberto, 17–18, 22, 50,
  128
editorial calendar, 52–3
editorialization, 23, 114–27
  definition, 115
Ellis, John, 24, 72, 134
emotion, 14–15, 44–5, 55,
  60–1, 81–7, 93–5, 101,
  117–19
  and news, *see* news
enunciative productivity, 84–7,
  134
escape, *see* pleasure
everyday life, 11, 14, 24, 52,
  59, 86, 97, 130, 136–7
extended family, 22, 45, 62–4,
  83
extrafilmic discourse, 4

fable, 23, 90–2, 108, 127, 133
Facebook, *see* social media
fairy tale, *see* fable
Feasey, Rebecca, 1, 31, 37, 83
feminine cultural community,
  86
feminist media studies, 10–15
film studios, 4
  decline of, 4–5
Fine, Jon, 3, 111
Fiske, John, 84, 121, 129,
  134–5
Frankfurt School, 11, 35
Fuller, Bonnie, 2–3, 25, 58,
  111, 114
  gossip's godmother, 2

Gamson, Joshua, 4–6, 15–16,
  68–9, 71–3, 87, 116,
  122, 128
gendered worlds of media, 27
Gill, Rosalind, 37
Goffman, Erving, 72

gossip:
  about celebrities, 86–7
  and consensus building,
    104–6
  and emotion, 85–6
  etymology, 83
  sociable nature of, 84–5,
    106–8
  social functions, 84, 104–8,
    133
guilt, 15, 22, 28, 37–43, 129–0
guilt shot, *see* photographs

Habermas, Jürgen, 29–33
Harper's Baazar, 94
heat, 83, 101
Hermes, Joke, 13–19, 27, 37,
    62, 83, 101, 122–3
Hilton, Paris, 32, 55, 72
Hobson, Dorothy, 12, 27, 35,
    39, 80
Holmes, Su, 1, 6, 68, 71
Huyssen, Andreas, 28–9

identification, 23, 31, 59–60,
    76, 79, 81–2, 87
  similarity identification, 60,
    81–2
intimate common world, 83
intimate public, 30–1
intimate sphere, 29–31, 34

Johansson, Sofia, 1, 31, 34, 39,
    83, 101
Jolie, Angelina, 46, 55, 82, 89,
    95
Jones, Deborah, 84, 133, 135
judgment, 14, 51, 102–3,
    127–8
"Just Like Us," *see*
  photographs

Kardashian, Kim, 46, 66, 81,
    122
Kardashian, Kourtney, 96–7

knowable community, 45,
    79–88
Kruger, Barbara, 66

Lai, Adrienne, 6, 71

McDonnell, Terry, 2
Marshall, P. David, 5, 33, 68
methodology, 16–21
  audience study, 19–21
  industry analysis, 18–19
  textual analysis, 17–18
  three-pronged approach, 16
Meyrowitz, Joshua, 72
Min, Janice, 3, 70, 114, 141
Modleski, Tanya, 26, 35,
    135–6
moral codes, 9, 89–98, 136
motherhood, 9, 90, 92–8, 127
  failed, 95
  heroic, 95–6, 124
  transformed transgressor,
    95–7, 125

Nash, Meredith, 934
news, 29–34, 107–115
  24-hour news cycle, 6
  celebrity news, 2, 32–3,
    111–14
  and emotion, 33–4
  human interest stories, 6,
    32–3
  "soft" news, 32–4
  news-stand sales, 3, 25, 110

"Octomom," 8–9
official culture, 12
oral culture, 84
ordinariness, *see* paradox of
  ordinary celebrity

paparazzi, 57–8, 69–71
parasocial relationship, 23, 79,
    82–3
People Magazine, 5, 49

PerezHilton.com, 132
photographs:
  beach bodies, 93, 102–3
  and the construction of
    fame: 67
  digitization, 55–6
  guilt, grief, and glory shots,
    117–19
  importance within celebrity
    gossip genre, 55–8
  "Just Like Us," 74, 78
  splice, 117, 119–20
  star at home: 78–9
  star-as-reader, 74–6
  visual proof: 62–3, 74, 94,
    116–20
Photoplay, 4
picture personalities, 4
Picture-Play Magazine, 4
pleasure:
  and academic research,
    9–11, 34–7
  admission of the reality of,
    14–15
  and audience, 14–15,
    128–30
  and escape, 10, 34, 59, 99
  and everyday life, 135–7
  false pleasure, 35
  guilty pleasure, *see* guilt
  and ideology, 13, 35
  and sociability, 83–4, 108,
    133–6
polls, 23, 63, 102, 127
popular feminine:
  contradictions, 12, 87–8,
    130
  definition, 25–6
  and female audiences, 27–31
  negative associations, 27–9
  and social change, 135–6
postfeminism, 37
pregnancy, *see* celebrity gossip
    magazines, narratives
privacy, 69–70, 98–100

private sphere, 31
public sphere, 29–33
purchasing magazines, 40–2,
    53, 130
puzzle solving, 122–3

radio, 5, 27, 32, 34, 67
Radway, Janice, 13–14, 16, 31,
    41
rationality, *see* reason
readership:
  and authority, 21, 108,
    114–16, 120–30
  feminine nature of, 22, 46–8
  hailing, 50, 59, 61–2, 77,
    79, 94
  male readers, 19, 42–3
  model reader, 50, 53, 61–4
reading public, 29
reason, 31–4
Rich, Frank, 112
Richie, Nicole, 9, 95
Rojek, Chris, 6
romance novels, 13, 26, 130,
    135

scandal, 4, 7, 91–3
schadenfreude, 100–3
scribbling women, 28
second-wave feminist
    scholarship, 12, 30
Silver Screen, 4
Simpson, Jessica, 8, 44, 105,
    115–16, 118
sincerity, *see* authenticity
skepticism, 16, 99, 112
soap opera, 26, 39, 43, 80, 86,
    130, 135
sociability, *see* pleasure
social media, 6, 68, 132
Spears, Britney, 44, 58, 92–4,
    100
stage work:
  back stage, 72–3
  side stage, 72–3

Steele, Michael, 53
Stone, Brittain, 55
studios, *see* film studios
surveillance, 37, 93–4, 98–9,
　103

tabloidization, 32–4
television:
　academic study of, 12, 27, 35
　cable, 6
　and intimate fame, 5, 67–8
　reality TV, 6, 66, 68
textual play, 121–4, 128–30
trash, 25–7, 38–40, 122
truth:
　ambiguous truthfulness, 113,
　　121–9
　truthiness, 113
Tumblr, *see* social media

Us Weekly:
　2004 magazine of the year,
　　3, 111
　circulation, *see* circulation
　transition to weekly, 2–3

Vanity Fair, 94
viewing tools, 116, 120, 127

W Magazine, 66
Wakeford, Dan, 47
weight, *see* body image
Wenner, Jann, 53
Wilkinson, Kendra, 46, 96–7
Williams, Raymond, 11, 80
Winship, Janice, 10, 12
working through, 133–7

YouTube, *see* social media